Cocaine

DRUGS The Straight Facts

Alcohol

Cocaine

Hallucinogens

Heroin

Marijuana

Nicotine

DRUGS
The Straight Facts

Cocaine

Heather Lehr Wagner

Consulting Editor
David J. Triggle
University Professor
School of Pharmacy and Pharmaceutical Sciences
State University of New York at Buffalo

CHELSEA HOUSE
PUBLISHERS
A Haights Cross Communications Company
Philadelphia

CHELSEA HOUSE PUBLISHERS

VP, NEW PRODUCT DEVELOPMENT Sally Cheney
DIRECTOR OF PRODUCTION Kim Shinners
CREATIVE MANAGER Takeshi Takahashi
MANUFACTURING MANAGER Diann Grasse

Staff for COCAINE

ASSOCIATE EDITOR Bill Conn
PRODUCTION EDITOR Jaimie Winkler
PHOTO EDITOR Sarah Bloom
SERIES & COVER DESIGNER Terry Mallon
LAYOUT 21st Century Publishing and Communications, Inc.

A Haights Cross Communications Company

http://www.chelseahouse.com

First Printing

1 3 5 7 9 8 6 4 2

Library of Congress Cataloging-in-Publication Data

Wagner, Heather Lehr.
    Cocaine / Heather Lehr Wagner.
        v. cm.—(Drugs, the straight facts)
Contents: Thinking about cocaine—A brief history of cocaine—How cocaine
affects your body—The business of cocaine—Who is really using cocaine?—
A look at addiction—Where to go for help.
    ISBN 0-7910-7260-6
    1. Cocaine habit—Juvenile literature. [1. Cocaine habit. 2. Drug abuse.]
I. Title. II. Series.
HV5810.W23 2003
362.29'8—dc21
                                                        2002155984

Table of Contents

The Use and Abuse of Drugs

The issues associated with drug use and abuse in contemporary society are vexing subjects, fraught with political agendas and ideals that often obscure essential information that teens need to know to have intelligent discussions about how to best deal with the problems associated with drug use and abuse. *Drugs: The Straight Facts* aims to provide this essential information through straightforward explanations of how an individual drug or group of drugs works in both therapeutic and non-therapeutic conditions; with historical information about the use and abuse of specific drugs; with discussion of drug policies in the United States; and with an ample list of further reading.

From the start, the series uses the word *"drug"* to describe psychoactive substances that are used for medicinal or non-medicinal purposes. Included in this broad category are substances that are legal or illegal. It is worth noting that humans have used many of these substances for hundreds, if not thousands of years. For example, traces of marijuana and cocaine have been found in Egyptian mummies; the use of peyote and Amanita fungi has long been a component of religious ceremonies worldwide; and alcohol production and consumption have been an integral part of many human cultures' social and religious ceremonies. One can speculate about why early human societies chose to use such drugs. Perhaps, anything that could provide relief from the harshness of life—anything that could make the poor conditions and fatigue associated with hard work easier to bear—was considered a welcome tonic. Life was likely to be, according to the seventeenth century English philosopher Thomas Hobbes, *"poor, nasty, brutish and short."* One can also speculate about modern human societies' continued use and abuse of drugs. Whatever the reasons, the consequences of sustained drug use are not insignificant—addiction, overdose, incarceration, and drug wars—and must be dealt with by an informed citizenry.

The problem that faces our society today is how to break

the connection between our demand for drugs and the willingness of largely outside countries to supply this highly profitable trade. This is the same problem we have faced since narcotics and cocaine were outlawed by the Harrison Narcotic Act of 1914, and we have yet to defeat it despite current expenditures of approximately $20 billion per year on "the war on drugs." The first step in meeting any challenge is always an intelligent and informed citizenry. The purpose of this series is to educate our readers so that they can make informed decisions about issues related to drugs and drug abuse.

SUGGESTED ADDITIONAL READING

David T. Courtwright, *Forces of Habit. Drugs and the making of the modern world*. Cambridge, Mass.: Harvard University Press, 2001. David Courtwright is Professor of History at the University of North Florida.

Richard Davenport-Hines, *The Pursuit of Oblivion. A global history of narcotics*. New York: Norton, 2002. The author is a professional historian and a member of the Royal Historical Society.

Aldous Huxley, *Brave New World*. New York: Harper & Row, 1932. Huxley's book, written in 1932, paints a picture of a cloned society devoted to the pursuit only of happiness.

David J. Triggle
University Professor
School of Pharmacy and Pharmaceutical Sciences
State University of New York at Buffalo

1

Thinking About Cocaine

Cocaine is a very addictive drug. Cocaine is a stimulant—it directly affects your brain. Cocaine stimulates certain nerve cells in the brain, producing feelings of intense pleasure. Users talk about feeling care-free, or relaxed, or utterly in control. But this artificial stimulation comes with a price tag. The "high" from cocaine lasts only from five to 20 minutes, and you will need more and more cocaine each time you try to match the feelings of that first, initial experience. Cocaine causes severe mood swings and irritability.

As soon as cocaine enters your bloodstream it goes to work, increasing your heart rate and raising your blood pressure. It increases your body's temperature and causes the pupils of your eyes to dilate. Repeated sniffing of cocaine powder causes your nose to become irritated and frequently runny. The cocaine can even eat away at the cartilage in your nose, producing holes.

No one starts out saying, "I want to be an addict." Cocaine is one of the most addictive drugs there is—both psychologically and physically. Once you use cocaine, even just one time, you cannot predict how much or how often you will continue to use it.

WHAT IS COCAINE?

Cocaine is a substance produced in the leaves of a shrubby bush that grows mainly in Peru and Bolivia. This bush, known as *Erythoxylum coca*, grows wild in parts of South America and is cultivated in others.

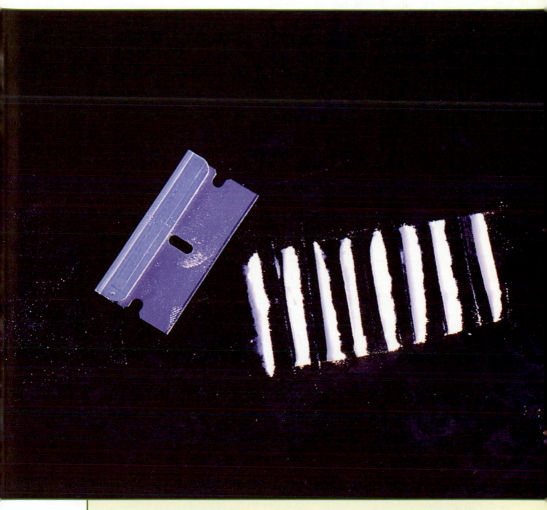

Cocaine is manufactured by heating a paste produced from the leaves of the coca bush with hydrochloric acid. The resulting white powder is often separated into fine lines and inhaled or snorted into the nose.

Cocaine is not a new drug. It is thought that the Incas were most likely the first to use cocaine, chewing the leaves of the coca bush more than a thousand years ago. The practice was originally reserved for priests in ceremonies and for soldiers and workers who relied on the simulating effects of the plant to increase their endurance. To this day, residents of the Andes Mountains where the coca bush grows still chew the leaves of the coca plant with little or no addictive effect. The amount of cocaine in the leaves, when chewed, is quite small, and the effect is similar to drinking several strong cups of coffee.

The absence of addiction among coca leaf chewers is supported by firsthand reports from researchers and biologists like Andrew Weil, M.D., who wrote in the *Journal of Ethnopharmacology*:

> I have lived among coca-using Indians of the Andes and the Amazon basin in Columbia and Peru and have not seen any signs of physical deterioration attributable to the leaf. I have never seen an instance of coca toxicity. Nor have I observed physiological or psychological dependence on coca. Even life-long chewers seem able to get the effect they want from the same dose over time; there is no development of tolerance and certainly no withdrawal syndrome upon sudden discontinuance of use.

However, this research does not imply that cocaine use is safe. The size of the coca leaf quid that can be chewed comfortably releases only a small amount of cocaine, much less than what is present in the powdered or crystallized form common to modern recreational use.

Cocaine as it is known today—in a synthesized form— was first isolated from the coca plant in 1855 by a German chemist named Albert Niemann. A paste is made from the leaves of the plant. Then this paste is heated with hydrochloric acid to produce cocaine hydrochloride. This is the most common form of cocaine: the white powder that is separated into fine lines, a few inches long, and then inhaled into the nose. When it is found in powder form, its purity can be anywhere from zero to 90 percent pure. In the form known as crack or "rock," it is generally 25 percent to 40 percent pure.

This element of uncertainty about cocaine's purity adds to

the risks inherent in using cocaine. You can never be certain exactly what is in that powder that you are inhaling. The dealer who supplied it will most likely have cut it with another substance to increase his or her profits. Cocaine may be cut with sugar, laxatives, cornstarch, talcum powder, or even amphetamines.

Rachel never planned to use cocaine. It just happened. Her family moved and she was in a new school. Some kids invited her to a party, and once the party started, she saw the lines of white powder on the shiny mirror. She wanted to fit in; she hated being the "new girl." She wanted these people to like her. So she tried it.

One of the boys must have known that she had never tried it before. He handed her a rolled-up ten-dollar bill. He told her to rub a bit of the powder on her gums, and then showed her how to inhale it.

At first, Rachel did not feel anything. But when it came, it was the most incredible feeling she had ever experienced. She felt completely comfortable and at ease, suddenly confident that she belonged. She felt energetic, capable of doing anything. All of her insecurities and anxieties disappeared.

She tried it several more times since that first party, and now she could hardly wait for the next opportunity. It was all she thought about. Regular life seemed boring and flat. It was simply the time that came before and after cocaine.

What Rachel may not know about cocaine is how it affects her brain. The confidence and energy she feels are caused by cocaine and its effect on the concentration of chemical messengers in her brain. She will quickly become accustomed to the neuronal imbalance that results in her confidence and energy, and she will need more and more cocaine to produce the same feelings.

This white powder may look clean and pure, but it is not. The once natural "high" the plant's leaves offered has become big business, and opportunities are used to cut corners and increase profits well before the cocaine reaches the dealer.

When the coca leaves are first harvested, they are thrown into pits, pounded or chopped, and then mixed with kerosene or gasoline as well as other chemicals. This process removes the cocaine from the leaves. This is the freebase form of cocaine, but it cannot stay in this form for long or it begins to lose its strength. In order to transport the cocaine, it is mixed with chemicals and converted into a kind of salt, which is less fragile and more easily transported.

HOW DOES IT AFFECT YOU?

Cocaine affects structures deep in the brain. Among these is the neural system located in the region of the brain known as the ventral tegmental area (VTA). This is one of the regions of the brain that, when stimulated, produces the sensation of pleasure. Nerve cells that begin in the VTA stretch down to the region of the brain known as the nucleus accumbens, which is one of the brain's key centers for creating feelings of pleasure.

When you are doing something that gives you pleasure, large amounts of dopamine—a neurotransmitter (chemical messenger) associated with creating these feelings of pleasure—are released in the nucleus accumbens by neurons that begin in the VTA. When your brain is functioning normally, a neuron releases this dopamine into the small gap between two neurons (known as the synapse). This dopamine then binds with specialized proteins, known as dopamine receptors, on the nearest neuron. When this happens, the dopamine sends a signal to that neuron, a signal that something pleasant is happening.

This is what happens when the brain is functioning normally, when you are doing something that makes you feel happy. When you use cocaine, though, it interferes with

This farmer in Peru harvests coca leaves, the base ingredient in cocaine. Cocaine production has a negative effect on the environment: 5.7 million acres of rainforest have been cleared to grow coca over the last 30 years in Peru alone, and 14,800 tons of toxic chemicals used in the production of cocaine paste have been dumped into the Amazon jungle.

this normal process. Research has shown that cocaine works by blocking dopamine from leaving the synapse. The result? A build-up of dopamine and an ongoing stimulation of the receiving neurons.

So what's so bad about that? What's wrong with feeling intense pleasure, even if it is an artificial feeling?

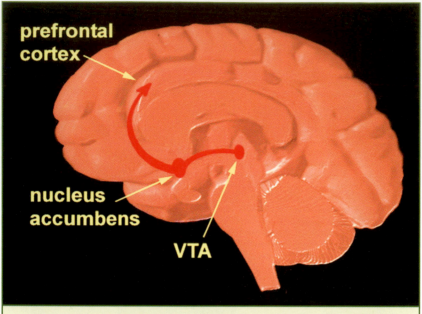

The reward pathway is a key concept in understanding the effects of drugs like cocaine on the brain. The reward pathway involves several parts of the brain, including the ventral tegmental area (VTA), the nucleus accumbens, and the prefrontal cortex. When activated by a rewarding stimulus like cocaine, a neurotransmitter called dopamine is released in the nucleus accumbens by neurons that begin in the VTA and then travels to the prefrontal cortex. The prefrontal cortex is a complex structure that influences cognitive processes like attention span, critical thinking, and expression of emotions.

When dopamine leaves the synapse, the signal that pleasure is taking place gradually disappears, and the process of nerve communication continues. When dopamine accumulates, for example with cocaine use, your brain grows accustomed to higher and higher levels of dopamine being present—not when something pleasant is going on, but simply as the brain's normal state. That means that you need to take more and more cocaine, and take it more and more often, to copy the "high" that you got the first time you used cocaine. It also means that when the dopamine is not present, your brain no longer feels as if it is in a normal state of functioning—it feels deprived. It requires the cocaine not simply to achieve a state of pleasure, but to make it seem as if everything is normal.

HOW COCAINE AFFECTS YOU

The pleasure cocaine brings doesn't last long. When snorted, the "high" lasts only about five to 20 minutes. The effects on your body last longer, and the long-term dangers of continued cocaine abuse are frightening.

In the short-term, cocaine increases your blood pressure and heart rate. It constricts your blood vessels, dilates your bronchioles (the tubes you use for breathing), and increases your blood sugar. That is only in the short-term.

COCAINE AND TEENS: The Numbers

The 2001 Monitoring the Future study analyzed drug use among American teens and young adults. Here are some of the statistics researchers discovered when interviewing teens about their cocaine use:

- Among eighth graders, 4.3 percent report trying cocaine at least once.
- Among tenth graders, 5.7 percent report using cocaine at least once.
- Among twelfth graders, 8.2 percent say that they have tried cocaine at least once.

The number of students saying that they have tried cocaine in the last month was much lower. Only two percent of all twelfth graders and a little more than one percent of eighth or tenth graders say that they have used cocaine within the past month.

[Source: *whitehousedrugpolicy.gov*]

In the long-term, cocaine damages many different parts of your body. It damages your heart, leading to disturbances in your normal heart rhythm—disturbances that can cause a heart attack. It damages your respiratory system, leading to chest pain or even respiratory failure. It damages your neurological system, leading to headaches or even seizures or strokes. It causes problems with your gastrointestinal system (the system that handles digestion), leading to nausea or abdominal pain.

Finally, cocaine damages you psychologically as well as physically. It can trigger depression, anxiety, sleep problems, or irritability. It can lead to paranoia or even convulsions. You may begin to hallucinate and gradually slip away from reality into a nightmare world.

M ark needed extra money. His cocaine habit was getting expensive. At first, he had only used it occasionally with friends. They had snorted it. Then one of his friends had introduced him to smoking it, and he quickly found it harder and harder to wait for the next time. He was doing it by himself now, and even though smoking it was less expensive, he was using more and more.

He had used up the savings from his summer job. Now he was taking money from his parents and his sister. It wasn't really stealing, he told himself. He would pay them back when he could. So he took a bit from his dad's wallet, a bit from his mother's purse, and a bit more from the allowance money his sister kept in an envelope in her dresser.

Mark is learning that cocaine will make you do things you never thought possible, like stealing from your family. When someone like Mark is addicted to a drug like cocaine, he or she will continue to seek drugs in spite of the negative consequences of his or her drug use.

MAKING WISE CHOICES

It is important to learn about any drug—what it is, where it comes from, and how it affects your body—before deciding to use it. Cocaine, whether snorted, smoked, or injected, is an illegal drug. Cocaine is highly addictive. It is expensive. It impairs your judgment. It interferes with your brain's under-standing of what creates pleasure, causing you to lose interest in all of the other areas of your life—your friends, your family, sports, and school.

In this book, you will read about teens making decisions about cocaine. You will learn more about how cocaine affects your body. You will learn about the legal issues surrounding cocaine and how laws governing cocaine have changed over the years. You will find out some surprising statistics about cocaine and learn more about the people most likely to use and abuse it. Finally, you will learn about how to deal with cocaine addiction, how to prevent problems, how to ask for help if you need it, and what to do if you suspect that a friend or family member is abusing cocaine.

This information will help you make wise choices when you are thinking about cocaine. Perhaps you have already tried cocaine or been at a party where it was offered to you. Maybe you have a friend or family member whom you suspect may be addicted. Through the stories of the teens in this book and the facts contained in each chapter, you will learn more about cocaine and begin to understand how it can affect you.

2

A Brief History of Cocaine

For the Incas who cultivated the coca bush in ancient Peru, the plant they were growing and harvesting was a critical part of religious ceremonies. Records show that the coca bush was grown in parts of South America as far back as 1000 A.D. and was viewed by those who tended it as a sacred symbol of endurance, strength, and even fertility. Its use was reserved for the most important members of Incan society: royalty and certain nobles.

In these early ceremonies, the leaves of the coca bush were chewed. The result was a mild stimulant, similar to drinking a few cups of strong coffee. Addiction was seldom a problem since each leaf contained only a very small amount of the drug.

Those who chewed the leaves experienced greater alertness and became less sensitive to hunger or cold. Eventually, small supplies of coca leaves were placed in storehouses along important routes so that they might be used by the kingdom's warriors or messengers.

In 1532, Pizarro's conquest of the Incas marked a new chapter in the use of the coca bush. Once reserved only for important ceremonies or for the use of select groups, the coca bush became a form of currency. The Spanish conquerors used coca plants as a kind of payment for the natives to ensure their cooperation and to keep them energized for the backbreaking labor they were required to perform.

Soon, missionaries from the Catholic Church became concerned by the effects of more widespread use and availability of

Pizarro's conquest of the Incas in the sixteenth century forever changed the use of coca leaves in Peru. Once reserved for Incan priests and soldiers, chewing coca leaves became widespread when Spanish conquerors used coca leaves as payments for Incan laborers. Eventually, the Spanish took over coca production and cultivation completely from the Incas.

the coca leaves, both for the natives and their conquerors. The coca leaves were symbolic of the Incan religion, and their use seemed to support a kind of worship the Catholic

Church wished to stamp out. In 1560, laws were passed to attempt to eliminate this new system of currency, but they proved short-lived. Soon, the new government set up by Spanish conquistadors took over the coca production and established a monopoly both on its cultivation and on its use as currency.

Spaniards carried the plant back to Europe, where it failed to generate much interst, most likely because the coca leaves had lost their potency during the long voyage from Peru. Centuries later, a German chemist named Albert Niemann from the University of Gottingen experimented with attempts to isolate the drug from the plant's leaf. In 1858, he succeeded.

Niemann's success would lead to the first widespread cocaine epidemic. Since the full extent of the drug's addictiveness was not known, cocaine soon gained use as a local anesthetic. Peru became the site of a network of German-owned plantations and factories, all attempting to cultivate the new "miracle drug." The Dutch also soon entered the competition, cultivating their own cocaine plants in Java—a variety that many felt was far superior to the German version.

Its use as a replacement for snuff (a powdered form of tobacco) resulted in cocaine being not only injected intravenously, but also inhaled into the nose. Its addictiveness was not yet widely understood, but this ignorance would not last long.

FREUD AND COCAINE

By the mid-1880s, commercial production of purified cocaine was a full-fledged industry. While many real and imagined uses for the drug were proclaimed, its most extensive medical use was as a local anesthetic in eye surgery.

In those early days of medicine, a rather horrifying prospect faced the patient needing the skills of an ophthalmologist (a doctor specializing in the structure, function, and diseases of the eye). When eye surgery was required, it was often necessary for the patient to be able to move his or her eye as the surgeon instructed—without pulling away or flinching! An Austrian ophthalmologist named Karl Koller was the first to discover that when cocaine was used as a local anesthetic, the patients were able to handle this grueling process and the surgery could be successfully completed.

Word of Koller's experiments soon spread. Other European physicians were proving equally resourceful at discovering new uses for cocaine. In 1883, a German doctor named Theodor Aschenbrandt discovered a new use for cocaine, this time a military one. Aschenbrandt prescribed cocaine to Bavarian soldiers during training and discovered that it helped them cope with fatigue and exhaustion during maneuvers.

The results of Aschenbrandt's military use for cocaine were published in a German medical journal, a journal that was read by a neurologist named Sigmund Freud. It would be Freud who would serve as one of cocaine's most prominent spokespersons. In July 1884, Freud published his own study of cocaine, titled *Uber Coca* [*On Cocaine*]. Citing the exhilaration and euphoria the drug induced, Freud came to the misleading conclusion that cocaine could be taken without any risk of addiction. He cited its potential medical uses as a mental stimulant, as an aphrodisiac, as a local anesthetic, and even as a treatment for everything from digestive disorders and asthma to a cure for morphine and alcohol addiction.

It did, of course, cure many addicts of their addiction to morphine or alcohol—they instead quickly became addicted to cocaine. Freud had advocated that cocaine be taken orally, a method that would have enabled some of the cocaine to be broken down in the liver before it reached the brain, resulting in a less intense experience of euphoria. But in the 1880s the use of the syringe was perfected, and soon hypodermic needles were more widely available. Morphine addicts quickly began injecting themselves with cocaine or cocaine mixed with morphine. It would be some time before Freud would be forced to admit that it was not hypodermic needles that caused cocaine to prove addictive, but the drug itself. By then cocaine was being used not only in wealthy European circles, but also among lower- and middle-class Europeans and even in America.

THE FIRST COCA-COLA

The idea of marketing a drink containing cocaine originated in France. A Corsican chemist created *Vin Mariani*, a wine containing small amounts of cocaine.

The success of Vin Mariani inspired American John Pemberton to create what he described as his version of the "French Wine of Coca, the Ideal Tonic." In 1886 Pemberton began to market his syrupy beverage, which consisted of a blend of coca leaves and African kola nuts—a drink that he labeled "Coca-Cola." Initially designed as a kind of medicinal beverage, Coca-Cola was sold in drugstores. Soon, soda fountains opened in drugstores across Georgia to offer customers a convenient place to purchase and consume the beverage. The new drink, and the soda fountain where it was dispensed, would quickly spread across the United States.

That same year, 1886, cocaine gained another important military endorsement, this one from Dr. William Alexander Hammond, the Surgeon General of the U.S. Army. At a meeting of the New York Neurological Society, he advocated the use of cocaine for medical purposes.

It would be several more years before the danger of cocaine and its addictiveness were fully recognized. In the early part of the twentieth century, many so-called "tonics" or medicinal beverages were sold to customers unaware of the danger they posed for addiction. These tonics, unregulated by any governmental agency, promised a wide range of miracle cures based on the ingredients they contained—cocaine and opium.

Americans would soon discover that there was little of the miraculous about these tonics. By 1902, estimates show that

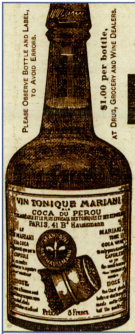

For Body and Brain.

SINCE 30 YEARS ALL EMINENT PHYSICIANS
RECOMMEND

VIN MARIANI

The original French Coca Wine; most popularly used tonic-stimulant in *Hospitals, Public and Religious Institutions* everywhere.

Nourishes   Fortifies   Refreshes

Strengthens entire system; most AGREEABLE, EFFECTIVE and LASTING Renovator of the Vital Forces.

Every test, strictly on its own merits, will prove its exceptional reputation.

PALATABLE AS CHOICEST OLD WINES.

Illustrated Book Sent Free, address:

MARIANI & CO., NEW YORK

A Corsican chemist created *Vin Mariani*, a wine containing small amounts of cocaine, in the late nineteenth century. The popularity of this drink prompted American John Pemberton to create Coca-Cola, a blend of coca leaves and African Kola nuts. Soda fountains dispensing this drink opened in Georgia and soon spread across the United States.

there were some 200,000 people addicted to cocaine in the United States. By 1903, responding to public concern, Pemberton agreed to remove cocaine from his Coca-Cola.

THE HARRISON NARCOTIC ACT

As concern about the growing numbers of people addicted to various drugs grew, and as a prohibitionist movement to ban alcohol gained popularity in various quarters throughout the United States, the government began to recognize the need for greater control and regulation of the distribution of these substances. In December 1914, the United States Senate approved the passage of the Harrison Narcotic Act under the urging of then Secretary of State William Jennings Bryan.

The bill was labeled an "act to provide for the registration of, with collectors of internal revenue, and to impose a special tax upon all persons who produce, import, manufacture, compound, deal in, dispense, sell, distribute, or give away opium or coca leaves, their salts, derivatives, or preparations." Rather than making opium or cocaine illegal, the Harrison Act instead allowed doctors and pharmacists to continue to prescribe narcotics, and manufacturers and importers to continue to meet this demand, provided that they registered with the internal revenue office and paid the fee of one dollar per year. (At the time cocaine was incorrectly labeled as a "narcotic.")

The law further said that government officials who were "lawfully engaged in making purchases" of these drugs were exempt from paying the tax. The manufacturers of tonics and potions containing small amounts of cocaine were also exempt, provided that the narcotic content of their products did not exceed a certain fixed amount.

The opportunity the Harrison Act offered to those seeking to stamp out the spread of addiction was contained in one small phrase. A doctor or a dentist was permitted to continue to prescribe cocaine and other narcotics, provided that it was done "in the course of his professional practice only." In other words, cocaine could be prescribed as part of a recommended course of medical treatment but not merely to help someone who was addicted to the drug avoid the symptoms of withdrawal or continue with their drug use. Doctors found to be writing prescriptions without some medical backup for the prescription could be and were arrested.

As a result, addicts who had previously had little problem obtaining their next fix legally and under medical supervision soon found that their supply had dried up.

Doctors were reluctant to write out prescriptions for these drugs for fear that they would be questioned by law enforcement officials and have their medical practices damaged by the ensuing publicity.

Rather than stamping out drug abuse, the Harrison Act prompted the gradual growth of an underground, illegal industry for supplying drugs. The Harrison Act did not stop people from using cocaine and other drugs; it simply forced them to look elsewhere for their supply. About three years after the Harrison Act was passed into law, a governmental committee was formed to look into its effects. They discovered that the illegal (or "underground") trade in drugs now was approximately equal to the legitimate sale; that smuggling routes had been set up at access points to the United States, particularly at the border with Canada; and that, based on reports from several American cities, drug use had actually increased since the Harrison Act had been passed.

It would not be the last time that the government and law enforcement authorities were forced to confront a burgeoning drug problem in the United States. The same questions that plagued leaders in the early part of the twentieth century continue to trouble lawmakers today. What effect has criminal legislation had on the drug problem? How can addicts be encouraged to seek help and ultimately recover from their addictions? How can the United States secure its borders against the smuggling of illegal substances?

A BRIEF LULL

Gradually, greater power was given to local law enforcement authorities to regulate drug trafficking in their communities. Public awareness of the dangers cocaine posed grew, and many of its earlier advocates were forced to acknowledge their own addictions. By the middle of the twentieth century, cocaine use had declined, and the period from the 1940s through the 1960s saw little mention of cocaine or concern about its abuse.

In the late 1960s, however, the climate had changed in the United States. Recreational drug use became more acceptable among young Americans. Popular culture soon celebrated a freer lifestyle, one linked with drug use. Drugs became a symbol of a new generation, a generation that rebelled against the values and power structures its parents and grandparents had embraced.

COCAINE IN AMERICA: A Timeline

1886: John Pemberton markets syrupy beverage consisting of a blend of coca leaves and African kola nuts, called "Coca-Cola." U.S. Army Surgeon General William Alexander Hammond advocates the use of cocaine for medical purposes.

1902: Statistics show 200,000 Americans addicted to cocaine.

1903: Pemberton agrees to remove cocaine from Coca-Cola.

1914: Harrison Narcotic Act passed.

1970: Controlled Substances Act passed.

1973: Drug Enforcement Agency created.

1981: Medellin cartel consolidates power.

1985: Crack epidemic in New York City draws media attention.

1986: Len Bias dies of a cocaine overdose.

1990: Panama leader Noriega is captured and taken to Florida.

1993: Pablo Escobar is killed.

1995: Cali cartel leaders arrested.

2000: President Bill Clinton approves $1.3 billion aid package to Colombia for combating drug trafficking.

[Source: *www.pbs.org/wgbh/pages/frontline/shows/drugs/*]

Drug use was no longer stigmatized. The drugs of choice in the 1960s were marijuana, LSD, and heroin. To help offer a more effective governmental response to the rise in drug use, President Lyndon Johnson created a new division of the Justice Department, the Bureau of Narcotics and Dangerous Drugs (BNDD). The BNDD was designed to consolidate responsibility for drug enforcement into a single agency, rather than the previously scattered system spreading enforcement duties among customs officials, law enforcement agencies, and other national agencies.

In October 1970, Congress passed the Comprehensive Drug Abuse Prevention and Control Act, a law designed to consolidate all previous drug laws regulating the manufacture and distribution of drugs. It gave law enforcement officials the right to conduct "no-knock" searches for drugs. The law is particularly significant for the fact that it contains the Controlled Substances Act which places all substances regulated under federal law into one of five categories. The categories are chosen based on the drug's medicinal value, harmfulness, and potential for abuse or addiction. Drugs placed in Schedule I are considered to be the most dangerous, with no recognized medical use. Drugs in Schedule V are considered to be the least dangerous.

Cocaine is listed as a Schedule II drug. This means that it is considered to have a high potential for abuse, and that abuse of cocaine may lead to severe psychological or physical dependence. However, its placement in this category indicates that it has a "currently accepted medical use in treatment in the United States or a currently accepted medical use with severe restrictions."

In 1971, President Richard Nixon declared that drug abuse was a public enemy and launched a governmental war on drugs. However, the approach under Nixon was significant and unique—the focus was on drug abuse prevention, with most funding going towards treatment rather than enforcement of drug laws. Two years later, President Nixon would announce the creation of a new agency to handle all aspects of the nation's drug problem: the Drug Enforcement Agency (DEA).

A NEW COCAINE PROBLEM

In November 1975, Colombian police seized a small plane at an airport in Cali, Colombia, after receiving a tip that it contained drugs. On board they found 600 kilos (1,323 pounds) of cocaine. It was the largest cocaine seizure that had ever been made up to that time. It also signaled to drug enforcement authorities, both in Colombia and in the United States, that the illegal trade in cocaine was much larger than they had previously suspected.

The loss of this shipment did not go without a response. The cocaine traffickers launched a brutal retaliation, in part to attempt to seek out whoever had tipped off police and to signal the full extent of their power. Over a single weekend, 40 people were brutally killed in the Colombian city of Medellin, an event that would become known as the "Medellin Massacre."

A subtle shift was underway. Cocaine, which had previously seemed to pose less of a threat than other drugs, was suddenly back. By 1977, it was visible at certain society parties and glamorous settings throughout the United States. Its high price tag gave cocaine a certain, supposed cachet—not everybody could afford it. Its presence, like expensive cars and designer clothes, became linked to a certain lifestyle, a lifestyle that was quickly popularized in the media.

COCAINE WARS

In 1979, a Colombian named Carlos Lehder purchased 165 acres of land on the island of Norman's Cay in the Bahamas. Lehder would use this strategic location as a way to transform the smuggling of drugs into the United States. Lehder masterminded an operation that relied on using small planes and landing them at Norman's Cay for refueling on the journey

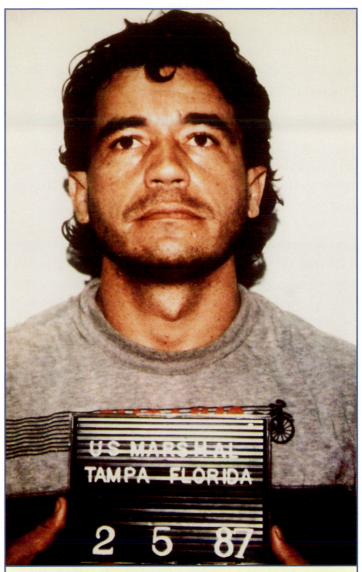

Carlos Lehder, shown here in a 1987 mug shot, and a group known as the Medellin cartel revolutionized the manufacture, smuggling, and distribution of cocaine in the United States. Estimates claim that the Medellin cartel was responsible for smuggling over 70 percent of the cocaine used in the United States in the early 1980s.

from Colombia to the United States. Lehder used bribes and intimidation to cement his position on Norman's Cay.

By 1981, Lehder and a group of other Colombians, including Pablo Escobar, Jose Gonzalo Rodrigues Gacha, and members of the Ochoa family, had united their drug operations into a single, powerful entity labeled the Medellin cartel. The cartel consolidated the various stages—manufacturing, distribution, and marketing of cocaine—and allowed its members to exercise even greater control and pose a more significant threat to law enforcement officials and local governments.

When the U.S. government was ultimately able to pressure Bahamian authorities to crack down on the Norman's Cay drug operation in 1982, the Medellin cartel formed a new alliance—this time with the leader of Panama, General Manuel Noriega. Noriega agreed to allow cocaine to be moved through Panama from Colombia, en route to the United States, in exchange for a payment of $100,000 per load. The deal had been negotiated by Noriega and Pablo Escobar. Escobar would further demonstrate his power that same year by being elected to Colombia's Congress. Escobar was elected on a platform that focused on bringing greater opportunity to the poor—he traveled through the slums of Medellin, accompanied by Catholic priests, and handed out money to poverty-stricken residents there. He would remain in office for only one year before being forced out by a reform-minded government.

Evidence of the increased trafficking in cocaine and the growing power of the Colombians became clear on March 9, 1982, when nearly 4,000 pounds (1,814 kilos) of cocaine were seized at Miami International Airport. The large size of the shipment—valued at more than $100 million—made it clear to U.S. drug enforcement officials how extensive the Colombian drug operation had become.

For much of the 1980s, cocaine became the drug of

choice of many wealthy and well-known Americans. Efforts to crack down on imports from Colombia would meet with minor victories and then new setbacks. As soon as one point of entry was eliminated, another would spring up. In the mid-1980s, drug enforcement officials based in Florida began to concentrate their efforts on shipments coming through Miami. The South Florida Drug Task Force's successes forced a major shift in the cocaine smuggling route—it was transferred to the 2000-mile border between the United States and Mexico. By the middle of the 1980s, most cocaine entering the United States would do so over this border.

Pressure was increased on the Colombian government to extradite known drug traffickers to the United States to stand trial. When Colombian officials finally agreed to begin this extradition process, they became a target. In 1985, a Colombian Superior Court judge was assassinated, other judges were routinely threatened, and the Colombian Palace of Justice was attacked, resulting in the deaths of 95 people including 11 Supreme Court justices. All paperwork concerning pending extradition cases was set on fire and destroyed.

A NEW EPIDEMIC

By 1985, it was clear that a new form of cocaine was causing an epidemic, particularly in New York City. In the early 1980s, the smokeable form of cocaine known as crack was developed and quickly spread. Its low cost and strong potential for addiction meant that cocaine no longer could be considered a drug for the wealthy. In the form of crack, cocaine was hooking an entirely new population—one that was often younger and poorer than previous groups of cocaine addicts.

Gradually, the image of cocaine began to grow tarnished. The death of Len Bias in 1986 dramatically illustrated the dangers of cocaine. Bias was a talented basketball player for the University of Maryland who had been selected as the second-round draft pick by the Boston Celtics. A mere two days after the triumph of the draft selection, Bias died from a cocaine overdose.

Previous media coverage had focused on cocaine as a glamour drug. With the death of Len Bias and the spread of crack, the coverage began to shift to the dangers of cocaine, the health hazards to people who used it, and its potential for addiction.

The U.S. government's efforts also began to shift—from targeting smugglers to placing equally forceful pressure on world leaders who enabled the smugglers to access the United States. In 1988, a new president, Carlos Salinas de Gortari, was elected in Mexico. U.S. president-elect George Bush made it clear in a meeting with Salinas that he expected the new president to do everything in his power to cooperate in U.S. efforts to fight drug smuggling.

For Bob, the best part of high school had been playing varsity football. He had been good, but then came a stupid injury his junior year, leaving him unable to play. It was during that year, when he was sidelined from football and worrying about whether or not he would make the team his senior year, that he first tried cocaine at a party. For the first time away from the football field, Bob felt powerful and confident. He felt the same thrill that he used to get on the brightly lit field Friday nights, when the announcer would call out his name over the loudspeaker and cheers would echo from the bleachers. It used to be playing football that made him feel good about himself. Now it was cocaine.

What Bob may not know yet is that cocaine is not an adequate replacement for the excitement and sense of accomplishment he misses in his life. It may help him recapture the feelings he had on the football field for a time, but eventually even those feelings will fade as his tolerance to cocaine increases.

That same year, a U.S. federal grand jury issued an indictment against the Panamanian leader Manuel Noriega. Noriega, it was charged, had cooperated with drug traffickers, allowing them to use his country to launder money as well as to build laboratories to process cocaine in Panama. On December 20, 1989, U.S. forces invaded Panama. Noriega avoided capture for more than three weeks by seeking asylum in the Vatican embassy. Ultimately, under pressure from drug enforcement officials, he was forced to surrender. He was flown to Miami to stand trial. On July 10, 1992, he was convicted of drug trafficking, racketeering, and money laundering and sentenced to 40 years in prison.

Throughout the 1990s, other drug kingpins would be hunted down. In December 1993, Pablo Escobar, one of the leaders of the Medellin cartel, was killed during a raid by Colombian police. In 1995, five leaders of the Cali cartel were captured. Other arrests would follow—in Mexico, in Ecuador, in Colombia, and in Venezuela—all designed to eliminate cocaine production facilities, close down potential money laundering operations, seize cartel leaders, and block potential smuggling routes.

THE WAR CONTINUES

Billions of dollars have been spent in the past decade in the war against drugs. The creation of new agencies to combat drug smuggling, the naming of new drug "czars" to direct the drug enforcement efforts, and the tougher sentencing for drug users and dealers have all underscored the seriousness with which this problem is viewed by leaders.

Yet cocaine is still available. According to the U.S. Drug Enforcement Agency, cocaine is the second most commonly used illicit drug in the United States. About ten percent of Americans over the age of 12 have tried cocaine at least once in their lifetime. About two percent have tried crack. And nearly one percent of all Americans are currently using cocaine.

The worldwide supply of cocaine is still controlled by organized crime groups, most of them based in Colombia. The U.S. border with Mexico remains the primary point of entry for cocaine shipments smuggled into America.

ARE YOU CARRYING COCAINE IN YOUR WALLET?

Drug trafficking generates a lot of money for drug dealers, and the United States spends close to $20 billion battling drug suppliers and educating the general public about the health problems associated with drug use in an effort to reduce demand. Cocaine and money are related in an even more direct way.

Studies in recent years estimate that a large percentage of U.S. currency, up to 80 percent, bears traces of cocaine. However, this does not mean that every contaminated bill has been used to snort cocaine or has come in direct contact with the drug. It only takes one cocaine-tainted bill to contaminate an entire cash register full of money. Considering the millions of automated teller machines, money sorting and counting machines, and cash registers in the United States, it is easy to see how quickly much of the country's currency would become contaminated with cocaine.

However, this contamination does not mean that the average American will get high or fail a drug test simply by handling contaminated cash. A study by the Argonne National Laboratory in 1997 revealed that the average amount of cocaine on a contaminated bill measures about 16 micrograms, or one-sixteen millionth of a gram. (As a comparison, the average recreational user snorts more than 3,000 times that amount to get high).

The contamination does call into question the validity of police searches and asset forfeiture based solely on trace amounts of cocaine on currency. U.S. courts are increasingly rejecting cocaine-tainted paper money as evidence that the owner of that money was involved in drug activity.

As discouraging as these facts are to those engaged in combating drug smuggling, there are some signs that law enforcement officials are encountering some small success in stemming the flow of cocaine into the United States. The Drug Enforcement Agency points to the declining purity of cocaine samples being seized from smugglers and dealers as an indication that the available supply of cocaine is decreasing. The purity level of cocaine in these seized samples declined from 86 percent in 1998 to 78 percent in 2001.

It is a small victory. As long as cocaine continues to bring prices ranging from $12,000 to $35,000 per kilogram and as long as there are people willing to buy, the war will continue.

3

The Health Effects of Cocaine

Let us begin with the basics. Cocaine is a stimulant—a stimulant that affects the central nervous system. Cocaine stimulates sections of the brain that produce feelings of energy and a sense of well-being. Users of cocaine report feeling more in control of themselves and the world around them, and more competent at whatever they are doing.

But these feelings are short-lived. They will last no more than an hour, and more typically anywhere from five to 20 minutes. This combination—powerful good feelings that only last a short while—helps make cocaine so addictive.

It is important to remember that drugs do not affect all people in precisely the same way. Cocaine will not even affect the same person in the same way each time he or she uses it. Cocaine will produce different effects depending on the environment in which it is taken, how it is taken (snorted, smoked, injected), how much is taken, how frequently it is used, etc. This is, of course, separate from the fact that cocaine may be cut with different substances that can produce very different effects.

Let us take a closer look at the different forms of cocaine to better understand how it affects the body.

HOW IT ENTERS THE BODY

As learned in previous chapters, cocaine is derived from leaves of the coca bush. The coca leaf contains about one percent cocaine.

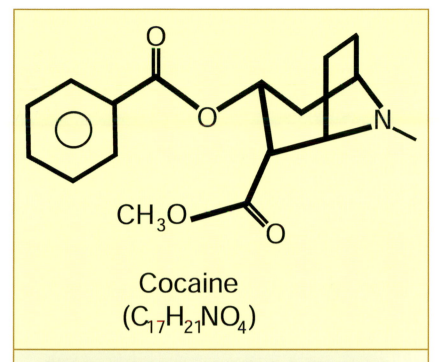

Cocaine
$(C_{17}H_{21}NO_4)$

This is the chemical structure of cocaine, $C_{17}H_{21}NO_4$, the most common form of the drug smuggled into and used in the United States. Cocaine in its natural state is an alkaloid, which is not easily dissolved. When it is converted to cocaine hydrochloride, it is easier to snort or inject.

In the most ancient and basic form of cocaine use, South American natives chewed the leaves of the coca bush to obtain a very mild effect, something similar to drinking a few cups of coffee. It also was a time-consuming stimulant, taking about 15 minutes before any effect was felt.

Beginning in the mid-1800s, researchers determined how to further refine this material into a substance that was nearly 100 percent pure powder. Cocaine begins in its natural state as an alkaloid. It cannot easily be dissolved, making it difficult to snort or inject. So hydrochloric acid is added, producing a substance—cocaine hydrochloride—that is highly water-soluble.

The majority of cocaine that is smuggled into the United States is in the form of cocaine hydrochloride.

Because of cocaine's composition, it cannot be taken in pill form like certain other drugs. The acids in the stomach do not degrade it, and it cannot be digested. The effects would not be quickly felt—there would be no sudden changed mood or increased energy.

Instead, cocaine is frequently taken by snorting through the nose. This route ensures a relatively short time between taking the drug and feeling its effects —approximately three to four minutes from nose to brain. The cocaine first penetrates the mucous membrane of the nose. From there, it travels into the veins and on to the right side of the heart. It is then pumped through the lungs, traveling on to the left side of the heart. From there, it proceeds to the brain, as well as the rest of the body.

The process is slightly different when cocaine is injected. Someone using cocaine might inject it into the arm using a hypodermic syringe. The cocaine would penetrate into the veins, then travel to the right side of the heart, through the lungs, and proceed on to the left side of the heart. From there, it would go on to the brain, a process taking approximately 14 seconds.

CRACK COCAINE

A separate form of cocaine is known as crack, or "rock." Crack is not injected or snorted; it is smoked through a pipe or other, similar device. This results in a much faster and more powerful high. When using crack, cocaine vapors are inhaled into the lungs. The cocaine avoids the right side of the heart and lungs and goes directly to the left side of heart and on to the brain, a process that takes no more than eight seconds.

The "high" produced by crack is much more intense than the high produced by cocaine, but its low is also much lower. Because the drug's effects are felt so quickly, and disappear so quickly, it is extremely addictive.

What is the difference between cocaine that is snorted or injected and crack? The powder or crystal form of cocaine—cocaine hydrochloride—cannot easily be converted into a gassy vapor. This would require extremely high temperatures—around 359°F (182°C)—temperatures high enough to destroy much of the expensive drug. To avoid wasting the cocaine in this way, an alternative route is to convert the cocaine hydrochloride back to its original alkaloid form, a

ATTITUDES AND BELIEFS: High School Seniors

How do most twelfth graders feel about cocaine and crack use? The U.S. Department of Health and Human Services' National Institute on Drug Abuse carried out a study of attitudes toward drug use among secondary school students. Some of what they learned:

- 84 percent of twelfth graders disapprove of people experimenting with cocaine.
- 88 percent of twelfth graders disapprove of people experimenting with crack.
- More than 64 percent of twelfth graders feel that people risk harming themselves if they try cocaine occasionally.
- 65 percent of twelfth graders feel that people risk harming themselves if they use crack occasionally.
- 90 percent of twelfth graders believed that their friends would disapprove of their experimentation with cocaine.
- 95 percent of twelfth graders felt that their friends would disapprove of their experimentation with crack.

[Source: Johnston, L.D., O'Malley, P.M. and Bachman, J.G. (2001) "Monitoring the Future: National Survey Results on Drug Use, 1975–2000." Vol. 1: Secondary School Students. (NIH Publication O. 01-4924) Bethesda, MD: National Institute on Drug Abuse] form at which it will vaporize at a lower temperature, 209°F (98°C). The term "crack" is thought to come from the sound that the cocaine makes when it is heated as it breaks down from a solid form into a gas that can be inhaled—a crackling sound that is actually burning bicarbonate.

Earlier attempts to break down the cocaine into a gas involved the use of ether and heat. Ether is highly flammable and heavier than air, and is used to free cocaine from impurities before it is heated and inhaled—a process known as "freebasing." However, ether is not easy to ventilate out of a room. Comedian Richard Pryor suffered a serious accident when attempting to light a freebase pipe while ether fumes were still in the room. Following reports of serious accidents involving the use of ether to freebase cocaine, the federal government began enacting stricter controls over its sale and distribution.

Crack is generally inhaled using either a water pipe containing liquid, in cigarettes, or in a straight, heat-resistant tube. This tube is particularly hazardous as it shoots unfiltered gas directly into the throat and lungs, neither of which is capable of tolerating heat that intense. Lung diseases like emphysema, normally seen in much older adults, can soon result from chronic use of crack cocaine.

There is no predictable amount of cocaine or particular form of its use that can be described as "safe." Cocaine, even in small amounts, even the first time you use it, can prove fatal. Some people have extremely violent reactions to cocaine the very first time they use it, and some even die. Your tolerance to the drug can change from one time to the next.

You may not know what is in the drug you are taking. Dealers use different techniques to increase the weight of the drug they are selling, thereby increasing their profits. Drain cleaner has been added to crack. The powder form of cocaine may contain PCP, amphetamines, caffeine, or simply some kind of white powder that looks like cocaine.

COCAINE IN THE BRAIN

A closer look at precisely how cocaine affects the brain is critical both to understanding how cocaine affects the central nervous system and why it is so addictive. Cocaine does not simply affect your brain; it actually *changes* your brain. How does this happen?

As we have learned, depending on the method through which cocaine is introduced into your body (either snorted, injected, or inhaled), the drug travels a quick route to its ultimate goal: your brain. In the brain, cocaine ultimately undergoes a critical transformation: from a source of pleasure to a desperate craving or need.

Your brain is constantly sending information and signals to your body, often without you even realizing it. For example, when you type on a computer keyboard, the signal for your finger to push the right key travels from your brain through your brain stem, down your spinal cord, and then through your hand to your finger. You are not aware that these signals are happening, but they involve a complex series of nerve impulses, traveling first as electrical signals, then chemical signals, and finally back as electrical signals.

These signals, or nerve impulses, are carried on part of their journey by substances called neurotransmitters, named for their ability to transmit information from one neuron to another. There are dozens of these neurotransmitters in your nervous system, each specifically developed to carry signals to certain cells called receptors. How does this work?

Think of your brain as a kind of elaborate message center. A message comes into your brain and is picked up by the dendrites. These branch-like parts of your brain gather up information coming in from sensory organs or even other neurons. Next, this information travels on to the axons, designed to relay messages from one neuron on to the next.

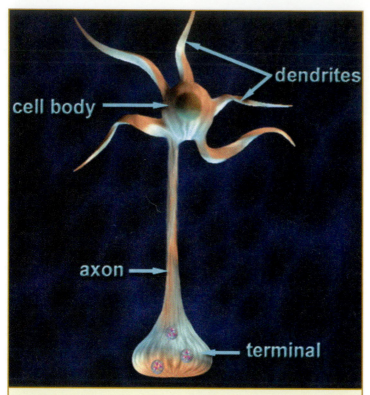

Dendrites on a neuron receive messages from other neurons, which are converted to electrical signals that travel toward the cell body. When the cell body receives enough electrical signals to excite it, a large electrical impulse is generated and travels down the axon toward the terminal. In the terminal area, chemical messengers called neurotransmitters are released from the neuron in response to the arrival of the electrical impulse. These neurotransmitters travel across the synapse to the next neuron, and the process repeats.

This message system does not work like a relay race, with one part of the system brushing up against another and then handing off the message. The pieces are not seamlessly attached, with messages traveling a straight path. Instead, there is actually a narrow gap between neurons—a gap so narrow that it is no more than one-millionth of an inch wide. This gap, called a synapse, poses an obstacle for the messenger attempting to get a message from one neuron to the next. The gap must be crossed. But how?

This is where the neurotransmitters enter the picture. The neurotransmitters are actually chemical substances, created and stored by the neurons until they are needed. Once the neuron receives the signal to carry a message on, the neurotransmitters are released. They jump across the synapse gap — or, more accurately, squirt across — and attach themselves to specially designated receptors on the other side. Each neurotransmitter has its own particular receptor. Some trigger an action response; others send a signal inhibiting a response.

THE PLEASURE PRINCIPLE

Neurotransmitters are the triggers for a number of bodily responses. Are you feeling sad? Sleepy? Anxious? Calm? These feelings are all triggered by neurotransmitters. There are many neurotransmitters at work in your body triggering certain feelings and sensations — everything from pain to pleasure. Scientists have currently identified about 75 neurotransmitters in the human body, and most believe that there are many more still to be identified.

Certain neurotransmitters are particularly sensitive to the presence of drugs in the body. Doctors frequently attempt to treat illnesses like chronic, severe depression with medication designed to trigger particular neurotransmitters.

When cocaine enters your brain, its target is the neurons containing the neurotransmitters known as dopamine. At least four major clusters of cells in the brain produce dopamine. What makes dopamine so critical to understanding cocaine? Dopamine is normally released by your brain when you are doing something you enjoy — playing with a pet, eating a delicious dessert, spending time with someone you care about, or walking on a beach.

Some drugs — like nicotine — work by triggering the release

of dopamine. Cocaine operates differently. Cocaine acts to block the dopamine transporter, the physiological mechanism by which dopamine (and many other neurotransmitters) are removed from the synapse to avoid prolonged action. Blockade of the dopamine transporter increases the concentration of dopamine in the synapse. This build-up of dopamine in the synapse results in an ongoing stimulation of the receiving neurons.

While this is a somewhat simplistic explanation of what is

Kevin was in the emergency room of the hospital. Two friends had dropped him off and then left him there. They were afraid—afraid of the strange way that Kevin was acting, and afraid that they would get into trouble. They had all been at a party, and some of the kids were using cocaine. Kevin had been one of them.

The next thing they knew, he was hunched over in a corner, rubbing his arms constantly, and acting as if he were seeing things that weren't there. He kept talking about flashing lights. He was sweating, and his skin was a strange red color.

They took him to the hospital because they were afraid of what was wrong with him. They left him there, alone, because they were even more afraid of what would happen when the doctors found out exactly what was wrong with him.

Kevin and his friends are learning that cocaine use can be costly. Some first-time cocaine users feel a rush of energy, confidence, and euphoria while others, like Kevin, have violent reactions. People vary in their ability to tolerate cocaine, and for some, even small amounts can prove harmful or even fatal. Experiencing the positive effects of cocaine once does not guarantee a similar experience in the future since tolerance to the drug can change over time.

a highly complicated process, it may help you to better understand cocaine's effects and its addictiveness. Cocaine's ability to block dopamine transporters results in an increased concentration of dopamine in the spaces between neurons. Your brain will quickly adapt to the increased amount of dopamine present in it. With regular cocaine use, the increased concentration of dopamine will become "normal." This means that you will need more and more cocaine to mimic the euphoric effects of those earliest experiments with the drug. In the same way that your brain will interpret the presence of cocaine as one of the most pleasurable experiences you can have, it will interpret the absence of cocaine as one of the most painful.

Recently, research carried out at Brookhaven National Laboratory in New York by Dr. Nora Volkow has demonstrated that there is a direct relationship between how intense and long-lasting a "high" from cocaine is and how extensively it blocks one of the key mechanisms that controls how much dopamine is in the brain. Because cocaine blocks dopamine's transporter sites, preventing the dopamine from completing its normal cycle and returning to the brain cells that released it, higher concentrations of dopamine remain in the brain. They stay there longer than they normally would. These high levels of dopamine make the cocaine user feel powerful and capable of doing just about anything.

So what is so bad about feeling good? Cocaine will cause your pupils to dilate, your blood vessels to narrow, your heart rate and blood pressure to increase, and your appetite to decrease. These physical symptoms all pose particular risks that we will discuss in greater detail later. For now, let us concentrate on what happens when cocaine blocks critical neurotransmitters from their preordained tasks.

Certain neurotransmitters are critical to your maintaining a normal state of mental health, i.e., what lies in between a "good mood" and a "bad mood." Frequent use of cocaine can make this "normal" state impossible to achieve.

cocaine

Cocaine creates a "high" by increasing the effective concentration of dopamine in the brain. It does so by targeting the neurons containing the neurotransmitter, dopamine. By blocking these transporter sites, cocaine causes the dopamine to remain in the brain for longer than usual, making the user feel euphoric, confident, and energetic.

When neurotransmitters are depleted by cocaine, you will feel intense anxiety and a chemically caused depression. Your body is signaling that the cocaine, which had artificially created your intense feelings of pleasure, has now disappeared, and there is nothing left to take its place. The extra dopamine manufactured to replace that which cocaine had blocked has now depleted your supply.

People who regularly abuse cocaine can so alter their brains that they no longer have the capacity to manufacture these critical neurotransmitters. They lose the ability to produce them naturally—they can only do it when cocaine triggers it. There is no more "normal" brain functioning: no more production of neurotransmitters to produce a good mood naturally. There is only intense craving for cocaine and the temporary relief that comes when the drug is once more present in the brain.

WHAT HAPPENS WHEN YOU QUIT COCAINE?

If cocaine alters the way your brain functions, changing the brain's ability to manufacture certain transmitters, what happens when you stop using cocaine? Can your brain change back to the way it was before you started abusing the drug?

The answer to this question offers both good news and bad news. Most experts in brain functioning believe that the changes created by lengthy cocaine abuse will alter the brain in certain basic ways. These changes may be permanent.

Research at the Brain Institute at the University of Florida has shown that, even months after cocaine use has stopped, there continue to be changes in the amount of dopamine receptors and transporters in the cocaine user's brain and how these receptors and transporters are functioning. However, because there will be certain parts of the brain unaffected by the cocaine, recovering addicts can hope to achieve sufficient brain functioning—provided that they give up cocaine permanently.

4

The Business of Cocaine

The business of cocaine begins in conditions of deep and lasting poverty, on remote farms in Colombia, Bolivia, and Peru. Along various points of the Andes Mountains, cocaine is transformed from a simple crop—the coca bush—into a highly profitable commodity. Those at the beginning of this transformation, the coca farmers, see little wealth from their crop. It is simply that cocaine has proved more profitable than some of the other crops they might produce, things like bananas or coffee.

Cocaine powder begins in Peru, where coca leaves, coca paste, and cocaine base are all produced. Along the eastern portion of the Andes Mountains, in the dense jungle of the Upper Huallaga Valley, one can find the largest single source of coca leaf in the world. Most estimates show that about 60,000 farmers depend on producing coca for their livelihood. The coca bushes can produce four harvests every year and thrive in an inhospitable climate and terrain that make growing other crops much more difficult. The farmers' hard work earns them a mere fraction of one percent of the retail value of the crop they harvest.

To increase their profits, many farmers have expanded their operations to include the producton of cocaine paste. The process is less than glamorous; the farmers take the coca leaves and stomp on them in their bare feet, then soak them in bleach or kerosene to yield the coca paste.

United States drug enforcement officials, working with the

Peruvian government, have attempted to address drug production at this initial source by offering farmers incentives to plant other crops. Their efforts have been largely unsuccessful. The presence of the *Sendero Luminoso*, a guerilla group known as

Mike first tried cocaine when one of the seniors on his basketball team offered it to him at a party at the end of the season. This senior was one of the best players on the team; if he was using it, Mike decided, there couldn't be anything too bad about cocaine. Mike loved the way cocaine made him feel; it made anything seem possible. He soon came to hate the way he felt when he wasn't high.

Mike began spending a lot of money on cocaine. He was using up all of the money from his after-school job, plus a lot of what he had saved to buy a car. Soon the friend who was selling him cocaine suggested that Mike might try selling some, too. It seemed like the perfect solution, plus a way to get his hands on more cocaine than he could afford to buy on his own.

It quickly became hard for Mike to control himself. The more cocaine he had, the harder it was to focus on anything but using it. He found ways to dilute the supply he was selling to other kids so that he could keep more for himself. Sometimes he cut the coke with baby powder or condensed milk, but it didn't really matter what he used as long as it was white.

Cocaine trafficking is big business, but unlike products sold by other businesses, drug dealers and the quality of the drugs they sell are not regulated. There is no guarantee that the cocaine bought from someone like Mike is pure or safe, or even cocaine. By the time cocaine reaches the average buyer, it has passed through the hands of numerous dealers. In order for each dealer in this chain to make a profit, they must cut the cocaine with another substance, thereby increasing the amount of the drug they are able to sell.

This Peruvian farmer pours gasoline over coca leaves, part of the process of making coca paste, which will eventually be converted into crystallized cocaine for sale in the United States, Europe, and elsewhere. Estimates show that close to 60,000 farmers in the Andes Mountains depend on coca cultivation for their livelihood.

the Shining Path, has added to the complicated politics of the region. This terrorist group has taken over much of the territory where coca bushes are cultivated, demanding payments from the peasant farmers in the region. Government officials sent in to find and destroy coca bushes are attacked and killed.

Bolivia is another important source of cocaine. While Bolivian cocaine production is somewhat smaller than that of Peru, the industry is more firmly entrenched in Bolivia, with connections to the military and upper class that date back to the late 1970s. The coca plants grown here are found mainly in the central part of Bolivia near the mountainous region of Chapare.

In Bolivia, cocaine production began to grow in the final quarter of the twentieth century, when landowners who had previously focused on farming soybeans and sugar or grazing cattle on their land instead turned their attention to the harvesting of coca plants. Control soon concentrated in the hands of a few powerful "families," who used coca produced locally, as well as paste imported from Peru, and transformed it into the 90 percent pure cocaine base that is then exported, principally to Colombia.

Government efforts to eliminate, or at least curtail, the drug trade have proved largely ineffective. Both Bolivia and Peru suffer from economic problems that have made it difficult for their governments to present farmers with an enticing alternative to the coca crop. While a small amount of money does go to the coca farmer, little of the profits generated from the finished cocaine make their way back to their country of origin. The wealth generated by cocaine is most often spent outside of Peru and Bolivia, deposited into foreign banks, or spent on investments. Some is used to bribe politicians and make local authorities look the other way.

The cocaine industry further cripples the economy because of the higher pay it offers farmers. Many decide to grow coca bushes rather than traditional foods, thus causing the prices of these crops to go up since fewer and fewer of them are readily available.

Beyond the farmers who grow the coca plants, the cocaine industry does offer other job opportunities. There is a demand for workers to produce the cocaine paste or refine it into powder. The labs where the cocaine is processed must be built and landing strips must be constructed to facilitate easy access to the hidden sources of the drug. The trails that lead from farm to lab to airfield must be guarded, which offers another potential source of employment for guards.

It is easy to see why the business of cocaine is more complicated than a buyer and a seller somewhere in America. In poorer countries, cocaine provides employment where it is badly wanted and money where it is desperately needed.

THE COLOMBIAN CONNECTION

While only a tiny percentage of the revenue from cocaine finds its way back to Peru and Bolivia, in Colombia the profit cocaine generates is more clearly felt. Colombia has maintained tight control over the later stage of the cocaine industry—the business of exporting cocaine powder.

Within Colombia itself, even tighter control over the cocaine business is maintained. At one time, a group of less than 10 organizations, known as cartels, regulated the cocaine industry—dictating supply and pricing and controlling approximately 90 percent of the world's cocaine business. Among the best known of these are the Medellin and the Cali cartels, each named after the city where they were based.

It is at this final part of cocaine's production that the greatest revenues are generated. Once the cocaine paste has been processed into powder, it follows a twisting network of routes (via road, boat, and air) to avoid law enforcement authorities. With profits to invest, smugglers are able to use top-of-the-line boats and airplanes—many with highly sophisticated navigation equipment.

At one time, southern Florida was the main entry point into the United States for cocaine arriving from South America. New York was the second port of choice for smugglers. More recently, the majority of cocaine entering the United States does so by crossing the Mexican border. From these entry points, the cocaine is then distributed to

This gunman from the Medellin cartel poses in Colombia in 2000. By maintaining tight control over the export of cocaine to countries like the United States, Columbian cartels dictated the supply and pricing, and reaped huge profits, from the cocaine business.

the U.S. cities where the majority of the cocaine business is based: New York, Los Angeles, San Francisco, Chicago, Houston, New Orleans, and Dallas.

OTHER COUNTRIES, OTHER CONNECTIONS

While much of the cocaine industry, from production to distribution, has been based in Peru, Bolivia, and Colombia, other nations have become involved in the distribution of cocaine. Smugglers transporting drugs from South America have targeted fuel stopover points in Panama, Nicaragua, Honduras, Jamaica, the Bahamas, Haiti, Cuba, and Mexico prior to entry into North America. Brazil, bordering on the three major cocaine-producing countries, has become a point of distribution in the drug trade. Brazil has also become a coca-producing nation. Coca farms in northwestern Brazil can easily transport their crops along the Amazon River and on to Colombia.

The industry has also spread to other South American nations, offering new points of transit from Colombia to North America and Europe. As drug enforcement efforts have attempted to crack down on shipments coming in from Colombia, smugglers have turned to Argentina and Venezuela, both for processing and export.

In fact, producers have been skillful at taking advantage of weak governments, officials susceptible to bribery, and remote locations with airfields somewhere between North and South America to further extend the network distributing cocaine. The industry is more than simply production and export. A key element of the profitability of cocaine lies in what happens to cocaine once it crosses over the borders of the United States.

For years, the island of Norman's Cay in the Bahamas was a center of drug smuggling activity for the head of the Medellin cartel, Carlos Lehder, as we have discussed earlier in this book. Located approximately 210 miles (338 kilometers) from

This map shows the main entry points through which cocaine enters the United States. Because the DEA has concentrated its efforts on stopping the influx of cocaine through Florida and the major cities on the East Coast, the majority of cocaine now entering the United States crosses over the Mexican border.

Florida, Norman's Cay was ideally situated for smuggling. Lehder was successfully able to use money and threats to dominate the island. The prime minister of the Bahamas, Norman Pindling, was believed to have accepted bribes in order to ignore Lehder's illegal activities. From 1978 to 1982, Lehder bought up extensive property on the island, building an airstrip, a home, and a hotel. Soon, small aircraft were frequently landing and taking off from the

Cocaine enters the United States in bricks, which are then cut up among dealers. This shipment of 515 pounds was seized in July 2001 from an oil tanker in San Francisco Bay and had an estimated street value of $4.5 million.

island under the protective eyes of armed guards on the beaches. It was several years before American authorities were able to put a stop to the flow of drugs from this nearby Bahamian point by increasing pressure on the local authorities and Bahamian government.

In recent years, U.S. drug enforcement authorities have concentrated their efforts on the smuggling routes that had carried cocaine from South America into the United States along the main entry points of the East Coast, principally southern Florida and New York City. As a result, new routes have been created by smugglers who carry cocaine from South America into the United States via Mexico. The Mexican border has now become the primary access point for cocaine entering the United States. Estimates show that nearly 65 percent of all cocaine entering the United States does so by crossing this southwestern border.

THE COCAINE MARKETPLACE

As it passes from locale to locale, the price of cocaine steadily rises. In Colombia, processed cocaine is available for an estimated $1500 per kilo. Once the drug enters the United States, its potential for profit skyrockets. A kilo of cocaine, for example, may fetch as much as $66,000 once it reaches American soil!

The drug frequently enters the United States bundled in packs containing 100-200 kilos (220-441 pounds). Dealers overseeing large markets buy these bundles, and then cut both the bundles and the cocaine itself to reduce the size of the packages and increase their potential profits by reducing the purity of the drug. The packs are sold to regional dealers—groups (sometimes gangs) who control specific parts of the country.

From there, the cocaine is again repackaged and re-cut for sale to local dealers. By now, the drug has passed through several successive handlers and has been re-cut to reduce its purity at nearly every stage. The local dealers often reduce the purity themselves before selling it to users. By the time it reaches the user, the end product often bears little resemblance to the highly concentrated cocaine powder that first crossed the U.S. border.

MONEY LAUNDERING

The vast profits of the illegal drug trade result in a problem for the drug industry: how to handle the money (generally cash) that cocaine generates?

The network that operates so efficiently in moving cocaine from the border to the street is equally efficient in moving money. Cash is collected from the local dealers and then transferred to a central collection point (the biggest are in southern

DRUGS AND TEENS:
In the United States and Abroad

In early 2001, an international study was published comparing the use of tobacco, alcohol, and illegal drugs by teens. The study covered 31 countries, including the United States, and surveyed 15- and 16-year-olds. The results included some of the following facts:

- Fewer American tenth graders smoke cigarettes than European tenth graders (26 percent compared to 37 percent said that they had smoked a cigarette in the past month).

- Fewer American tenth graders drink alcohol than their counterparts in Europe (40 percent compared to 61 percent said that they had consumed alcohol in the past month).

- However, more American 15- to 16-year-olds admitted to smoking marijuana at least once in their lifetimes (41 percent of American tenth graders compared to an average of 17 percent for European students).

- The numbers are also higher for cocaine use. Eight percent of U.S. tenth graders say that they have used cocaine at least once, compared to one percent in Europe.

- Four percent of U.S. tenth graders say that they have tried crack at least once. The rate of crack use among all European tenth graders was found to be two percent or less.

[Source: "Monitoring the Future: National Survey Results on Drug Use, 1975-2000." Illicit drug data from European School Survey Project on Alcohol and Drugs posted on *www.monitoringthefuture.org*, maintained by the University of Michigan Institute for Social Research]

Florida and New York City on the East Coast, Houston and Los Angeles on the West Coast). The cash is then "laundered"— disguising its source by converting it into legitimate revenue. Cash can be used to purchase money orders or cashier's checks, payable to a person who then deposits them in a bank account. From this account, the money is then transferred to another bank, either American or foreign. Businesses may be set up as "fronts" and drug money added to the businesses' own profits to disguise the source of the money and then enable it to be transferred elsewhere.

The cash most often ends up in "safe haven" countries, i.e., countries where banking laws protect depositors and enable them to avoid detection or having their financial activities reported. The Cayman Islands, located approximately 150 miles (240 kilometers) south of Cuba in the Caribbean Sea, are a favorite choice because of their bank secrecy laws.

5

Teenage Trends and Attitudes

According to the Centers for Disease Control (CDC), the use of cocaine is once again increasing among young Americans. Each year, the CDC surveys more than 13,000 high school students from around the country to determine their use of illegal substances.

The most recent study, surveying students for the year 2001, shows that the number of teens who said that they had tried cocaine in their lifetime increased to 9.4 percent. This shows a substantial increase over the high school students surveyed ten years earlier; in 1991, only 5.9 percent said that they had tried cocaine in their lifetimes.

The number of high school students reporting recent use of cocaine also is increasing. In 2001, 4.2 percent of high school students said that they had used cocaine in the past month, compared with 1.7 percent in 1991.

The U.S. Department of Health and Human Services also performs an annual survey of high school students to determine trends in their use of illegal substances. These annual results are published in a volume entitled *Monitoring the Future*. According to the most recent *Monitoring the Future* data, eight percent of all American tenth grade students say that they have used cocaine, and four percent say that they have tried crack.

These figures disturb public health officials, who are concerned that these increases reflect an ignorance of the health risks and the potential for addiction cocaine and crack pose. A

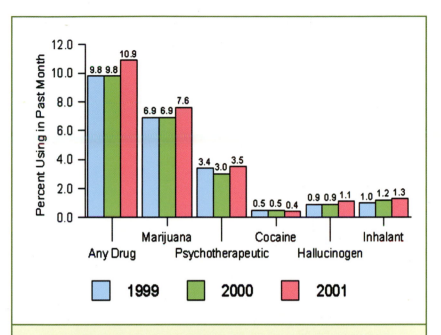

This graph from the 2001 National Household Survey on Drug Abuse shows the rate at which various drugs, including cocaine, were used among 14- to 15-year-olds over the past month for the years 1999, 2000, and 2001. The data from this survey, as well as surveys from the CDC and *Monitoring the Future*, all show similar trends: cocaine use continues among teens despite warnings about its negative health effects.

quick glance at the trends in cocaine use over the past few decades show that its popularity and the number of teens abusing the drug rose and fell depending on perceptions of the drug.

Results from surveys of high school seniors in previous *Monitoring the Future* studies show that cocaine use among seniors substantially increased from 1976 to 1979. In 1976, six percent of all high school seniors said that they had used cocaine. By 1979, that number had doubled to 12 percent. This figure remained relatively stable for the next five years, increased slightly in 1985, and then leveled again in 1986.

As we have learned in previous chapters, the mid-1980s brought a shift in public perception of cocaine, as well as how it was portrayed in the media. Greater awareness of the hazards of cocaine use produced a drop in the numbers of high school seniors using cocaine. From 1986 to 1992, the number of high school seniors who said that they had used cocaine at least once in the previous year decreased from 12.7 percent to 3.1 percent. The number who said that they had used cocaine in the previous month decreased from 6.2 percent to 1.3 percent.

The numbers then rose again in the late 1990s—in fact, they doubled. By 1999, 6.2 percent of high school seniors said that they had used cocaine in the past year; 2.6 percent said that they had used it in the previous month. Researchers had found some hope in the fact that 2000 figures showed a decline to five percent, but one year later the figures were once more rising.

CRACK: The Numbers

The data on crack use and abuse among high school seniors dates back to the mid-1980s, when references to crack were generally available only as part of a larger, comprehensive picture of cocaine use. However, rather than referring to crack specifically by name, information about its abuse was more commonly reflected in questions about smoking cocaine.

Between 1983 and 1986, the number of high school seniors who reported that they had smoked cocaine in the past year more than doubled—from 2.4 percent to 5.7 percent. An increase was also clear in the number who said that they had tried to stop using cocaine in the past year and been unable to stop, as well as in those who reported active daily use of cocaine. These numbers are all thought to reflect the spread of crack in the mid-1980s.

By 1987, surveys contained specific questions about crack. By this time, the media had also painted graphic portraits of

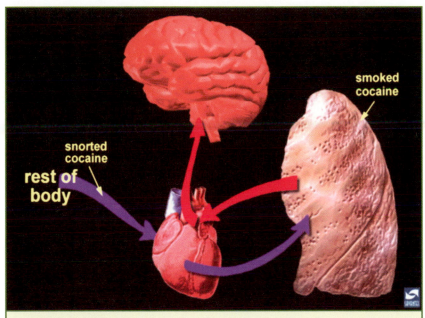

smoked
cocaine

snorted
cocaine

rest of
body

Smoking the crack form of cocaine delivers the drug to the brain more quickly than does snorting. Snorting requires that the cocaine travel from the blood vessels in the nose to the heart (blue arrow), where it gets pumped to the lungs (blue arrow) to be oxygenated. The oxygenated blood (red arrows) carrying the cocaine then travels back to the heart where it is pumped out to the organs of the body, including the brain. Smoking bypasses much of this process—the cocaine goes from the lungs directly to the heart and up to the brain. The faster an addictive drug reaches the brain, the more likely it will be abused.

crack abuse—showing the ravages of crack on whole communities from the addicts to their babies, born premature and addicted. Tougher drug sentencing also contributed to a different attitude toward crack and cocaine.

In studies measuring drug use among high school seniors, the period from 1986 to 1991 shows a sharp decline in crack use, from 4.1 percent to 1.5 percent. The prevalence of crack use then stayed level for several years before once more rising between 1993 and 1999 (an increase from 1.5 percent to

2.7 percent). A decline to 2.2 percent in 2000 has since been offset by increasing figures reported in 2002.

While it is helpful to see how the number of high school students who say that they have used cocaine or crack have increased and declined over the years, these figures offer an incomplete picture of exactly who is using cocaine. They are, in the end, only numbers. A more complete picture includes real people who have made choices that have impacted real lives.

PORTRAIT OF A COCAINE USER

Teens decide to use cocaine for a variety of reasons. It is rare to find a teen who snorted, smoked, or injected cocaine with the hope of becoming addicted. They use cocaine because they want to feel better about themselves, and cocaine offers a quick fix, an instant "high." They try it because they want to fit in with a particular group. They try it because they have heard rumors of the drug's benefits: it will help them feel more confident, lose weight, or have more energy.

For some teens, cocaine can be a gesture of independence, a way to signal that no adult can take away their right to make their own decisions. It may be a way to "break the rules."

Teens may be influenced to use cocaine in subtle ways. It may be a scene in a movie, a story in a magazine, or an image on television. Even though cocaine is illegal, many movies depict popular actors and actresses using the drug in a way that makes it seem acceptable, conveying a sense that people who use cocaine are somehow more sophisticated, more glamorous, or "edgier" than those who don't.

There are other factors that may mark a teen's likelihood to use drugs. Teens with poor grades and low self-esteem are more likely than their peers to use drugs. Teens from single-parent families are more likely than their peers to abuse cocaine and other illegal substances. Teens who have suffered abuse, who have grown up in a violent household, or in a household where a family member suffered from mental illness or substance abuse problems or had been jailed, are more likely to become substance abusers themselves. Few teens who do use cocaine are unaware of the risks. They like the way cocaine makes them feel and they view its hazards as something that could happen when they are older or if they use the drug for many years. They believe that they will easily be able to stop before they reach the point where cocaine will seriously damage their health. They believe that they can easily stop before they become addicted. They are wrong.

Traci's friends called it snowball or blow. Her boyfriend called it nose candy. Traci didn't worry about names. Her boyfriend had brought some to her house a few weeks ago so that she and her friends could try it. It was the greatest thing Traci had ever experienced, and she couldn't wait to do it again. She and her friends had pooled together some money so that her boyfriend could buy more, and they had had another party over the weekend. Every time Traci thought about the party, every time she talked to her friends, she remembered the feeling the cocaine had given her. She wanted to feel that way again. It was as if there were a tiny voice in the back of her mind, whispering to her, nagging at her, reminding her of how much better she could be feeling.

According to the CDC, Traci's pattern of cocaine use is becoming more and more common among teens. In 2002, 9.4 percent of teens admitted to trying cocaine in their lifetime, compared to only 5.9 percent in 1991. Regular use of cocaine is on the rise as well, with 4.2 percent of teens admitting they had used cocaine in the past month in 2001, compared to 1.7 percent in 1991.

The prevalence of negative images of cocaine and crack use in the media, such as this picture of police raiding a crack house in Washington, D.C., have done little to affect the overall trends of cocaine use among teens. Peer influence and reinforcement from the positive effects of the drug itself seem to overshadow scare tactics and education.

WHAT TEENS REALLY THINK ABOUT COCAINE

Despite new information about the risks of cocaine use and greater data about precisely how cocaine affects the body, teens continue to try cocaine. Technology has made it possible for scientists to observe the changes that happen in the brain when someone uses cocaine. They can see the way the brain is affected by each stage: the initial "rush," the "high" and then the absence of the drug that sparks a craving for more. Scientists are even able to identify the parts of the brain that become active when a cocaine addict see or hears something that sparks their craving for cocaine.

Even with all of this information available, cocaine remains a serious problem. According to the National Institute on Drug Abuse, more than a million Americans over the age of 11 are chronic cocaine users.

You may already have your own ideas about cocaine, based on information you've read in this book, learned from other sources, or even heard from friends or family members. What do other teens think about cocaine?

The National Center on Addiction and Substance Abuse (CASA), based at Columbia University in New York, surveyed 2,000 teens and 1,000 parents. The results of this survey offer a comprehensive picture of what teens think about drugs and how substance abuse has impacted their lives.

According to CASA, 60 percent of all teens are at moderate or high risk of substance abuse. That's 14 million teens aged 12 to 17!

What places a teen at risk for abusing drugs? The CASA study placed in this category any teen who had friends who used marijuana or friends who drank regularly, had a classmate or friend who used cocaine or heroin, felt that they could buy marijuana quickly, or answered that they expected to use an illegal drug in the future.

Where do teens rank cocaine? According to CASA's survey, cocaine is the third most often used drug by high school students (following marijuana and LSD/acid). Middle school students ranked it as the second most often used drug after marijuana. Nearly all teens surveyed agreed that cocaine use generally followed marijuana use—teens who smoked marijuana were more likely to go on to use cocaine than those who didn't.

There were other results from the CASA survey that show that teens admit that drugs pose a problem, both inside and outside school. If it sometimes feels to you as if everybody is using drugs, take a look at these results:

- 60 percent of teens said that they did not expect to use any drug in the future.

- 44 percent of teens said that they attended a drug-free school.

- 40 percent of teens said that the drug situation in school is getting worse (a decrease from the 55 percent who felt this way one year earlier).

THE STRAIGHT FACTS

Cocaine is an addictive stimulant that directly affects your brain. It interrupts the neurotransmitter balance in your central nervous system. This may give you a temporary feeling of increased confidence, greater energy, and a feeling of intense pleasure, but this will not last. Cocaine raises your blood pressure, increases your heart rate, causes your muscles to tense and your breathing to become more rapid. Use it regularly, and you will become paranoid, anxious, and confused. You may experience hallucinations. You may have trouble sleeping, easily become agitated, or become depressed.

It is as if cocaine is leaving a bill behind, and it is an expensive one. The cost of those initial feelings of confidence, satisfaction, energy, and well-being come after the cocaine leaves your system. Use cocaine as many people do—in a binge lasting a night or a few nights—and your body will ultimately crash. Sleep off the results, and you will soon face a body demanding more cocaine. Cocaine is highly

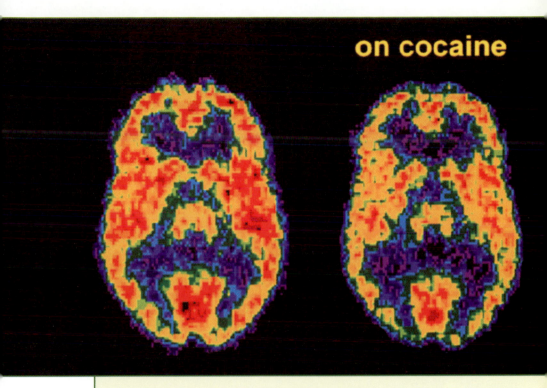

on cocaine

In addition to activating the brain's reward circuitry, cocaine affects the overall level of brain activity in the user. Scientists can observe cocaine's effect on brain functions using such sophisticated brain imaging technologies as positron emission tomography scanning (PET). PET scans allow scientists to see which areas of the brain are active by measuring the amount of glucose, the brain's main energy source, that is used by different brain regions. The left scan is taken from a normal, awake person. The red color shows the highest level of glucose utilization (yellow represents less utilization and blue indicates the least). The right scan is taken from someone using cocaine. The loss of red areas in the right scan compared to the left (normal) scan indicates that the brain is using less glucose and therefore is less active. This reduction in activity results in a disruption of normal brain functions.

addictive—you can become addicted very quickly after your very first cocaine experience. Cocaine use leads to nosebleeds, a constantly irritated nose, feelings of fear and paranoia, and an empty wallet.

The numbers show that many teens are making wise choices. They are choosing not to use cocaine—in fact, more than 90 percent of all teens have never tried it.

There are some basic steps you can take to stay drug-free. First and most important is remembering to make your own decisions, to worry less about what other people think of you and more about how you want to think of yourself. You can choose to surround yourself with people who are not using drugs. The friends who are around you can support your choices or make them harder. If you

WHAT TEENS SAY ABOUT COCAINE

According to the U.S. Department of Health and Human Services' *Monitoring the Future* survey of high school students, teens have strong opinions about cocaine:

- Between 85 and 90 percent of all high school seniors say that regular use of cocaine and crack poses a serious risk to the user.

- More than half of all high school seniors say that trying cocaine or crack once or twice is very risky.

- A survey of tenth graders shows that the majority view cocaine and crack as very dangerous.

- 84 percent of all high school seniors say that they disapprove of people experimenting with cocaine.

- 88 percent of all high school seniors say that they disapprove of people experimenting with crack.

[Source: Johnston, L.D., O'Malley, P.M., and Bachman, J.G. (2001). "Monitoring the Future: National Survey Results on Drug Use, 1975–2000." Volume 1: Secondary School Students. NIH Publication No. 01-4924. Bethesda, MD: National Institute on Drug Abuse] spend a lot of time just hanging out with your friends and feeling bored, find an after-school activity that you enjoy, a sport or a club, or volunteer at a shelter or food bank in your area. Find someone you trust and can talk to—a parent, a teacher or counselor, a pastor or friend—and share your questions and concerns.

At the back of this book, you will find resources, web sites, and organizations that can supply you with additional information about cocaine.

6

Cocaine Addiction

Addiction can be defined as a state in which you have given your-self over to something, made yourself dependent on this object or substance. Depending on who you are talking to, and what you are discussing, addiction can be viewed quite differently and thought to mean very different things.

There is a physical element to addiction, and this is the one we often think of first when discussing drugs and addiction. When speaking of a physical addiction to drugs, you will most often mean the body's dependence on a particular drug like cocaine. The body has built up a certain tolerance to the continued presence of a drug, and its absence causes intense physical suffering. The body may suffer symptoms of withdrawal—physical signs that the body is in distress because of the absence of a particular drug. This is the body's way of sending a clue that it has come to expect certain quantities of a drug at certain times, and the absence of the drug is now creating problems for proper function-ing of your body's systems.

There is also a psychological aspect to addiction. This is where phrases like "learned behavior" are often used. Someone who is addicted to drugs has developed a certain set of behaviors in response to particular situations. For many, drugs are a coping mechanism for certain emotional states like depression, loneliness, stress, or even fatigue. When an addict develops a particular pattern of behavior in response to these feelings,

Cocaine is a powerfully addictive drug. Addiction can be physical and cause the user to experience withdrawal symptoms when he or she does not use the drug. Addiction can also be psychological, and used in a pattern of behavior that helps the user cope with difficult emotions. An often overlooked aspect of cocaine addiction is its social aspect—that is, the user may associate certain friends and situations with drug use.

in other words, when he or she feels stressed or depressed, he or she takes drugs. The earliest stages of those feelings trigger a desire to use the drug to cope with that uncomfortable emotion.

There is even a social aspect to addiction. If you regularly take drugs with a particular group of friends, or in a particular setting—after a football game on Friday nights, when you are hanging out after school, etc.—simply being in that setting or with certain people can trigger a desire for the drug. This is why people battling addictions must often completely separate themselves from their old friends and drastically change their patterns of behavior. They need to avoid the settings and people who remind them of drugs.

COCAINE AND ADDICTION

Cocaine is thought to be one of the most powerfully addictive of all drugs. Its effects are long-lasting, and cocaine addiction involves physical, physiological, and social aspects.

For many years, the full scope of cocaine's addictiveness was not understood. The body's clues that it has become addicted—the symptoms of withdrawal from cocaine—are not as obvious as in other addictive drugs. Things like trouble sleeping, changes in energy levels, and increased depression are not always clear and can be explained by a variety of other factors.

It is important to remember that addiction involves a change in behavior—a change in which things that used to be important are forced to take a back seat to one particular behavior. What does this mean? In the case of cocaine, an addict will begin to give cocaine a higher priority than other things: higher than work or school, higher than sports and activities, higher than friends and family.

One theory states that there are seven factors that will indicate whether or not someone is dependent, or addicted, to a drug. They are:

1. Becoming aware that you need to take a drug, generally as a result of trying to stop

2. Wanting to stop taking drugs

3. Having a clear and specific pattern of drug-taking behavior

4. Experiencing symptoms of tolerance and withdrawal

5. Using the drug to avoid symptoms of withdrawal

6. Getting the drug becoming more important than anything else

7. Staying away from the drug for a brief period of time, only to quickly slip back into taking it again

COCAINE: The Warning Signs

If you think that cocaine is somehow safer than other drugs or are feeling curious about trying it, take a look at what people who regularly use cocaine say:

- "I need to use cocaine in order to feel okay."

- "I can't really predict whether or not I'm going to get high."

- "I need more cocaine than I used to in order get high."

- "Cocaine is the only way I can deal with stress."

- "Cocaine is the only way I can get through a day."

- "I used to use cocaine with friends, but now I only want to be alone when I get high."

- "I am having trouble at school and at home."

- "I promise myself I won't use any more, but I can't stop."

- "I feel alone."

- "I feel miserable."

- "I feel scared."

[Source: *www.pbs.org.wnet/closetohome/*]

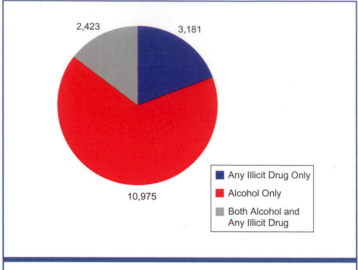

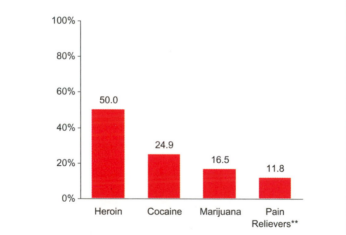

These two graphs from the 2001 National Household Survey on Drug Abuse illustrate current rates of addiction among teen drug users. The pie graph reports the estimated numbers of past-year drug users, aged 12 and older, who report an addiction to alcohol, an illicit drug (like cocaine), or alcohol and an illicit drug together. The bar graph shows the percentages of past-year drug users reporting an addiction to a specific drug; 24.9 percent of past-year drug users reported an addiction to cocaine.

Other experts explain the signs of addiction as the "Three Cs":

- Continuing to use cocaine, even though you know it is harming you

- Feeling a Compulsion to take cocaine

- Feeling that your cocaine use is out of Control

DO YOU HAVE A PROBLEM WITH COCAINE?

The National Council on Alcoholism and Drug Dependence has developed a test to help you determine whether or not you may have a problem with drugs. Portions of this self-test have been adapted here to help you honestly assess whether or not you may need help with your use of cocaine. Remember that only a professional—a doctor or trained specialist—can diagnose addiction. This list of possible risk factors for cocaine addiction is not designed to do that. Instead, it is designed to help you honestly examine your use of cocaine and better understand your risk factors for becoming dependent on cocaine.

Possible Risk Factors for Cocaine Dependency

- You use cocaine to build self-confidence

- You ever get high immediately after you have a problem at home, work, or school

- You ever miss school or work due to cocaine

- It bothers you if someone says that you use too much cocaine

- You started hanging out with a crowd that regularly uses drugs

- Cocaine is affecting your reputation

- You feel guilty after using cocaine

- You feel more comfortable or at ease at parties or on dates if you are using cocaine

- You have gotten into trouble at home, school, or work for using cocaine

- You borrow money or give up other things to buy cocaine

- You feel a sense of power when you use cocaine

- You lost friends since you started using cocaine

- Your friends use less cocaine than you do

- You use cocaine until your supply is all gone

- You wake up and wonder what happened the night before

- You have ever been arrested or hospitalized due to cocaine use

- You avoid lectures or speeches about cocaine use

- You have tried to quit or to cut back using cocaine

- Someone in your family has an alcohol or drug problem

- You think you might have a problem with cocaine

The National Council on Alcoholism and Drug Dependence suggests that identifying with three of these risk factors indicates that you may be at risk for developing a dependence on cocaine. If you identify with five or more of these risk factors, you should immediately seek professional help. Talk to a counselor, a nurse, or doctor. There are also organizations listed in the Yellow Pages of your phone book that can refer you to trained professionals who specialize in dealing with cocaine addiction and drug dependence.

DEPENDENCE VERSUS ABUSE

Is there a difference between abusing cocaine and being dependent on it? Most experts feel that there is. The American Psychiatric Association publishes a guide to mental health that contains specific guidelines to help its members properly diagnose cocaine abuse and dependence. This guide, known as the *Diagnostic and Statistical Manual of Mental Disorders* (DSM), describes cocaine abuse as happening when the user: (1) continues to use cocaine in spite of the adverse consequences; and (2) continues to use the drug in situations where it poses a physical danger. According to the DSM, cocaine abuse exists if at least one of these two factors applies to the user and if the user does not qualify as dependent on cocaine.

Tony would never admit it to any of his friends, but when he was alone, he felt afraid. The first couple of times he had used cocaine had been great—the most unbelievable feeling he had ever known. But after those first few times, it had never felt quite as intense. Still, he kept using and hoping that he would feel that way again.

But now it seemed that the cocaine didn't make him feel great—it just made him feel okay. It was as if being high had become normal. He kept thinking about cocaine—the smallest things would trigger this sense that he had to have more. He had used up all the money from his after-school job, he had even taken money from his mom's purse, and it wasn't enough.

And now he felt worried and afraid. Did his mom know that he had taken the money? Did his coach suspect that he was high at practice? What would happen when they found out? Most of all, he worried about the terrible way he felt. He was only 17 years old—he couldn't be an addict. Could he?

The fear that Tony feels is a combination of his realization that he may be addicted to cocaine, and the psychological and physical effects of cocaine itself. Heavy, regular use of cocaine is known to cause restlessness, anxiety, paranoia, and irritability, as well as insomnia and weight loss.

So what is cocaine dependence? The same DSM describes cocaine dependence as occurring when: (1) the user takes more cocaine than he or she intended to; (2) the user cannot reduce his or her drug use despite trying to; (3) the user spends a lot of time buying, using, and withdrawing from cocaine; (4) when being high or withdrawing from cocaine is interfering with daily life; (5) when activities involving cocaine are taking the place of all other social, school-related, and work-related activities; (6) the user continues to take cocaine in spite of the negative consequences; (7) the user needs to take more cocaine to get the same effects; (8) the user experiences withdrawal symptoms; (9) the user takes cocaine to self-medicate or to fight off the symptoms of withdrawal. You are considered to be dependent on cocaine if at least three of these nine factors apply.

IS SOMEONE YOU CARE ABOUT ABUSING COCAINE?

Cocaine abuse is not selective—it does not only happen in certain neighborhoods, in certain schools, or among a certain class or category of people. Drug abuse happens everywhere.

And addicts can look very much like the people around you. In fact, you may have picked up this book because you are concerned about someone around you—a friend or family member.

It can be quite difficult to tell if someone you care about is using cocaine. There are certain clues, warning signs that may indicate that cocaine or another illicit drug may be causing a problem:

- A change in friends

- A change in eating habits

- A change in sleeping habits

- Red, bloodshot eyes

- A runny nose

- Frequent sniffing

- A change in grades

- A change in behavior

- Acting tired or depressed

- Becoming careless about the way he or she looks

- No longer caring about family, school, or activities he or she used to enjoy

- Frequently needing money

It is important to remember that these are merely clues that cocaine or other drugs may be a problem. Only trained professionals can accurately diagnose a drug problem.

You cannot force a friend or family member to admit that they have a problem with cocaine or force them to stop—they have to do that themselves. However, there are certain things you can do to help someone you care about who is abusing cocaine. The first thing you can do is talk to someone you can trust about your friend's problem—perhaps a counselor, a teacher, a doctor, or a parent. Ask him or her to keep what you are sharing confidential. You don't even need to mention your friend's name. Adults can often provide you with additional resources or information that may be helpful as you decide what to do next.

If you decide to talk to the person you believe is abusing cocaine, think carefully in advance about what you want to say and when you want to say it. Pick a time when the person is not high. Don't use word like "addict" or blame him or her for using drugs; instead, express your concern about the drug use. Tell him or her how worried you feel, and what you've seen when he or she has been using cocaine—specific things you've seen him or her do or say that bothered you. Make it clear that you are talking to him or her because you care.

Be prepared that your friend or family member may

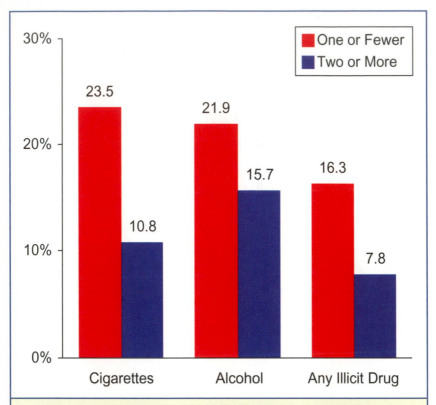

	One or Fewer	Two or More
Cigarettes	23.5	10.8
Alcohol	21.9	15.7
Any Illicit Drug	16.3	7.8

Studies have shown that students who use drugs, cigarettes, or alcohol are less likely to participate in extra-curricular activities. This graph shows the results of a 2000 report by the National Household Survey on Drug Abuse. Notice that students aged 12–17 are less likely to participate in more than one activity if they use or abuse drugs or alcohol.

become angry, make excuses, or deny what you are saying. Stress that you are speaking because you are worried. Offer to go with him or her to get help.

HELP IS AVAILABLE

At the end of this book we will talk about resources and treatment options that are available for people who have become addicted to cocaine. There are also certain groups and organizations that specialize in helping family members and friends of addicts. These groups can offer you support and advice. Your phone book will contain a list of local organizations that specialize in issues surrounding drug abuse. Your school nurse and counselor will also have information about support groups.

There are certain national organizations that may also have chapters or groups that meet in your area or may be able to provide you with information or even support. Some groups specialize in helping teens.

POINTS TO REMEMBER

Cocaine is illegal. It affects your brain and your body. Cocaine may make you feel carefree, relaxed, and in control, but that feeling will last only a few minutes. Use it enough and you will feel depressed and irritable. You will want more cocaine—and you will need to take more each time you want to get high. You won't eat or sleep regularly. It will increase your blood pressure and heart rate. It may cause convulsions or muscle spasms. Snorting cocaine can permanently damage your nasal tissue. It will also make you feel angry, hostile, paranoid, and anxious—even when you're not high.

Now take a look at crack. Crack may give you a quick high and a complete sense of power and pleasure. It is almost instantly addictive. It can lead to a fatal heart attack—even if you've only used it once. It can cause insomnia, seizures, hallucinations, and paranoia.

The highs from cocaine or crack last only a few minutes. The consequences last much longer. Think about this: there are more hospitalizations per year caused by crack and cocaine use than any other illegal drug.

7

Exploring Additional Resources

In this book we have discussed how cocaine can affect your body. We have learned a bit about the history of cocaine use, particularly in the United States. We have examined the business of cocaine, how the cocaine industry has grown, and how political efforts to control the drug industry have evolved.

We have read about teens making decisions about cocaine and learned more about who is likely to abuse cocaine and why. We have discussed cocaine addiction and learned what to do if you or a friend or family member needs help with a cocaine problem.

There are many resources available if you need assistance, support, or just more information about cocaine. Start with the adults you know—a parent, a teacher, your school counselor, a minister, or your doctor or nurse may be able to provide support or suggestions for places where you will find the help you need. There are also a number of organizations that specialize in dealing with drug-related issues, offering support groups, counseling, or helpful statistics and information. Many of these may have local chapters in your area—you can check your phone book to find one near you.

The day started out like any other. Julie woke up from partying all night and decided to do a couple of lines to get her day started. A couple turned into 5, then 6. By the time she was ready to go to her dealer for another few grams, it was raining and the roads were especially slick. But she had driven high before, so she wasn't worried.

As she drove across the bridge into the city, she lost control. The car started bouncing across the lanes like a ping-pong ball, hitting both cement medians over and over again. She felt the strain of the seatbelt crushing her chest and the impact of the airbag hit her in the face like a punch. Did the car finally stop? . . . Was she dead? . . . She could feel the blood running down her face and dripping onto her shirt.

Julie knew she had hit rock bottom as she sat in the emergency room, sore and bruised, but alive. She needed help. When the doctor offered to have a drug counselor speak to her when she felt better, she accepted. She and her parents met with the counselor and came up with a plan to help her kick her cocaine habit. The counselor mentioned that there were even support groups she could join where other teens with drug problems met to share their stories and offer each other support.

Julie is starting to realize that it is often difficult, or impossible, to beat an addiction without help. Parents and teachers are good places to start—and although they may be upset that you are using drugs, they will be relieved that you are seeking help. In addition, addiction counselors and organizations, such as Cocaine Anonymous and others listed in this chapter, can give cocaine addicts the support and direction they need to recover.

African American Family Services

Telephone: 1-612-871-7878

www.aafs.net

Provides referral services for substance abuse issues, including contacts for local treatment centers, support groups, family counseling, prevention, and diagnosis.

American Council for Drug Education

www.acde.org and *www.drughelp.org*

The American Council for Drug Education sponsors DrugHelp, a private, non-profit source of information and referral network. DrugHelp provides information on specific drugs and treatment options, and offers referrals to public and private treatment programs, self-help groups, family support groups, and crisis centers throughout the United States.

Cocaine Anonymous

Telephone: 1-800-347-8998 (for referrals to local meetings)

www.ca.org

An organization for cocaine addicts seeking to lead a life free from cocaine abuse. Members support each other in their effort through regular meetings held throughout the United States. Groups follow a 12-Step Program. Web site offers links to local chapters.

Co-Anon Family Groups

Telephone: 1-800-898-9985

www.co-anon.org

An organization for friends and family members of cocaine addicts. Offers information about addiction, support services and links to local meetings.

Girls and Boys Town National Hotline

Telephone: 1-800-448-3000

www.girlsandboystown.org

Offers tips, information, resources, and a chat room about family relationships, depression, violence in the family, and substance abuse. Trained counselors are on staff and can make referrals to specialists in your area.

TREATMENT TRENDS

There were nearly 1.9 million admissions to publicly funded substance abuse treatment programs in 1995:

- Nearly 46 percent of treatment admissions were for illicit drug abuse treatment, and 54 percent were alcohol abuse treatment.

- The largest number of illicit drug treatment admissions were for cocaine (38.3 percent), followed by heroin (25.5 percent) and marijuana (19.1 percent).

- Seventy percent of individuals in treatment were men, 30 percent were women.

[Source: National Association of State Alcohol and Drug Abuse Directors (NASADAD)]

Hazelden Information Center
Telephone: 1-800-257-7800
www.hazelden.org
Provides information and resources for teens and adults dealing with alcohol addiction and drug abuse. Also maintains treatment centers for those struggling with addiction.

Narcotics Anonymous World Services Office
Telephone: 1-818-773-9999 (for meeting information)
www.wsoinc.com
Narcotics Anonymous is an organization for recovering addicts. Members support and learn from each other in their efforts to live a clean and sober life following the 12-Step Program. Meetings are held throughout the United States and worldwide. Web site offers information, free publications, and links to local chapters.

National Clearinghouse for Drug and Alcohol Information
Telephone: 1-800-729-6686
www.health.org
Operated by the Federal Center for Substance Abuse Prevention, this organization provides a wide range of free information and resources on drug use and abuse, including material from the National Institute on Drug Abuse, the National Institute of Alcohol Abuse and Addiction, and more.

National Council on Alcoholism and Drug Dependence
Telephone: 1-800-NCA-CALL (1-800-622-2255)
www.ncadd.org
Provides public education and information on drug abuse and alcoholism. Also offers referrals to local treatment services.

BEATING COCAINE ADDICTION: A New Approach

Researchers at the Xenova Group, a biotechnology company in England, are in the process of creating a vaccine that will help cocaine addicts fight their addiction.

The euphoria associated with cocaine abuse occurs because cocaine blocks dopamine uptake in the brain, increasing the effective concentration of dopamine in synapses between neurons. The vaccine, called TA-CD, is designed to work by generating antibodies in the bloodstream that prevent cocaine from crossing from the bloodstream into the brain. In this way, the cocaine will not be able to block dopamine uptake in the brain.

This vaccine would be a novel therapy for cocaine addicts, who have had to rely on counseling, support groups, and willpower to beat their addictions. Cocaine addicts may benefit from TA-CD and its ability to inhibit them from feeling "high," and thus reinforcing their addiction, should they relapse after stopping cocaine use. NIDA is supporting the Xenova Group's development of this drug, which is still in early trial stages.

National Institute on Drug Abuse

Telephone: 1-301-443-1124

www.nida.nih.gov

The National Institute on Drug Abuse, a division of the U.S. Department of Health and Human Services, provides information on prevention and treatment of drug abuse. A special section for students contains research information about the effects of drug abuse on the brain and interactive activities to teach more about various drugs and how they affect how your brain works. It also features links to interesting information about the work that other scientists at the National Institutes of Health are doing.

Substance Abuse Mental Health Services Administration

Telephone: 1-800-662-HELP (1-800-662-4357)

www.samhsa.gov

A division of the federal government that offers drug and alcohol treatment referrals. Provides advice and information about local drug and alcohol treatment services, as well as links for teens.

Appendix

The Economic Cost of Drug and Alcohol Abuse in the United States

The National Institute on Drug Abuse (NIDA) and the National Institute on Alcohol Abuse and Alcoholism (NIAAA) released a study in 1998 that estimated the total economic cost of drug and alcohol abuse to be $245.7 billion for 1992, the most recent year for which sufficient data were available. This estimate represents $965 for every man, woman, and child living in the United States in 1992. Of this cost, $97.7 billion was due to drug abuse.

When considering the total cost of drugs and their impact on society, it is necessary to consider more than just the money spent on the drugs themselves. The NIDA/NIAAA estimate includes substance abuse treatment and prevention costs as well as other health care costs, costs associated with reduced job productivity or lost earnings, and other costs to society such as crime and social welfare. The study also determined that these costs are borne primarily by governments (46 percent), followed by those who abuse drugs and members of their households (44 percent).

The 1992 cost estimate has increased 50 percent over the cost estimate from 1985 data. The four primary contributors to this increase were:

- The epidemic of heavy cocaine use

- The HIV epidemic (spread by intravenous drug use)

- An eightfold increase in state and federal incarcerations for drug offenses

- A threefold increase in crimes attributed to drugs.

More than half of the estimated costs of drug abuse were associated with drug-related crime. These costs included lost productivity of victims and incarcerated perpetrators of drug-related crime (20.4 percent); lost legitimate production due to drug-related crime careers (19.7 percent); and other costs of drug-related crime, including federal drug traffic control, property damage, and police, legal, and corrections services (18.4 percent). Most of the remaining costs resulted from premature deaths (14.9 percent), lost productivity due to drug-related illness (14.5 percent), and healthcare expenditures (10.2 percent).

The White House Office of National Drug Control Policy (ONDCP) conducted a study to determine how much money is spent on illegal drugs that otherwise would support legitimate spending or savings by the user in the overall economy. ONDCP found that, between 1988 and 1995, Americans spent $57.3 billion on drugs, broken down as follows: $38 billion on cocaine, $9.6 billion on heroin, $7 billion on marijuana, and $2.7 billion on other illegal drugs and on the misuse of legal drugs.

Economic Costs of Alcohol and Drug Abuse in the United States, 1992 (millions of dollars)

Economic Costs	Total	Alcohol	Drugs
Health Care Expenditures			
Alcohol and drug abuse services	$9,973	$5,573	$4,400
Medical consequences	$18,778	$13,247	$5,531
Total, Health Care Expenditures	*$28,751*	*$18,820*	*$9,931*
Productivity Effects (Lost Earnings)			
Premature death	$45,902	$31,327	$14,575
Impaired productivity	$82,201	$67,696	$14,205
Institutionalized populations	$2,990	$1,513	$1,477
Incarceration	$23,356	$5,449	$17,907
Careers in crime	$19,198	-	$19,198
Victims of crime	$3,071	$1,012	$2,059
Total, Productivity Effects	*$176,418*	*$106,997*	*$69,421*
Other Effects on Society			
Crime	$24,282	$6,312	$17,970
Social welfare administration	$1,020	$683	$337
Motor vehicle crashes	$13,619	$13,619	-
Fire destruction	$1,590	$1,590	-
Total, Other Effects on Society	*$40,511*	*$22,204*	*$18,307*
Total	**$245,680**	**$148,021**	**$97,659**

Bibliography

Print

Blum, Richard H., ed. *Society and Drugs. Vol. 1: Social and Cultural Observations*. San Francisco, CA: Jossey-Bass Inc., 1970.

Chatterjee, Sumana. "More young people using illegal drugs, survey finds," *The Philadelphia Inquirer*, September 6, 2002, p. A4.

Cooper, Mary H. *The Business of Drugs*. Washington, D.C.: Congressional Quarterly, 1990.

Flynn, John C. *Cocaine*. New York: Birch Lane Press, 1991.

Johnston, L.D., P.M. O'Malley, and J.G. Bachman. *Monitoring the Future: National Survey Results on Drug Use, 1975–2000. Vol. 1: Secondary School Students*. Bethesda, MD: National Institute on Drug Abuse, 2001.

Karch, Steven B. *A Brief History of Cocaine*. Boca Raton, FL: CRC Press, 1998.

Kassin, Saul. *Psychology*. 3rd ed. Upper Saddle River, NJ: Prentice-Hall, Inc., 2001.

Lee, Rensselaer W. *The White Labyrinth: Cocaine and Political Power*. New Brunswick, NJ: Transaction Publishers, 1989.

Nahas, Gabriel G. *Cocaine: The Great White Plague*. Middlebury, VT: Paul S. Eriksson, 1989.

National Institute on Drug Abuse. *Cocaine and A Changing Brain: Meeting Summary, October 25, 1997*. Rockville, MD: National Institute of Health, 1999.

Nuckols, Cardwell C. *Cocaine: From Dependency to Recovery*. 2nd ed. Blue Ridge Summit, PA: Tab Books, 1989.

Platt, Jerome J. *Cocaine Addiction: Theory, Research, and Treatment*. Cambridge, MA: Harvard University Press, 1997.

Schaffer, Howard J. and Stephanie B. Jones. *Quitting Cocaine: The Struggle Against Impulse*. Lexington, MA: Lexington Books, 1989.

Weil, Andrew. "The Therapeutic Value of Coca in Contemporary Medicine." *The Journal of Ethnopharmacology*, 3 (1981) 367–376.

Wisotsky, Steven. *Beyond the War on Drugs*. Buffalo, NY: Prometheus Books, 1990.

Web sites

The National Center on Addiction and Substance Abuse at Columbia University
www.casacolumbia.org

In Search of the Big Bang
www.cocaine.org.uk

The Council on Alcohol and Drugs Houston
www.council-houston.org

The Church of Scientology International
www.drugfreelife.org

Schaffer Library of Drug Policy
www.druglibrary.org/schaffer/history/e1910/harrisonact.htm

Drug Strategies
www.drugstrategies.org

Go Ask Alice
www.goaskalice.columbia.edu

PREVLINE: Prevention Online
www.health.org

Join Together Online
www.jointogether.org

Monitoring the Future
www.monitoringthefuture.org

National Institute on Drug Abuse
www.nida.nih.gov

National Criminal Justice Reference Service
www.ondcp

Frontline: Drug Wars
www.pbs.org/wgbh/pages/frontline/shows/drugs/

Teen Challenge
www.teenchallenge.com/main/drugs/

U.S. Drug Enforcement Administration
www.usdoj.gov/dea/

Office of National Drug Control Policy
www.whitehousedrugpolicy.gov/drugfact/cocaine

Further Reading

Books

Cooper, Mary H. *The Business of Drugs.* Washington, DC: Congressional Quarterly, 1990.

Flynn, John C. *Cocaine.* New York: Birch Lane Press, 1991.

Johnston, L.D., P.M. O'Malley, and J.G. Bachman, *Monitoring the Future: National Survey Results on Drug Use, 1975-2000. Vol. 1: Secondary School Students.* Bethesda, MD: National Institute on Drug Abuse, 2001.

Lee, Rensselaer W. *The White Labyrinth: Cocaine and Political Power.* New Brunswick, NJ: Transaction Publishers, 1989.

Nuckols, Cardwell C. *Cocaine: From Dependency to Recovery.* 2nd ed. Blue Ridge Summit, PA: Tab Books, 1989.

Papa, Susan. *Addiction.* Farmington Hills, MI: Blackbirch Press, 2001.

Web sites

Cocaine Anonymous
www.ca.org

The National Center on Addiction and Substance Abuse at Columbia University
www.casa.columbia.org

Co-Anon Family Groups
www.co-anon.org

Freevibe.com
www.freevibe.com

PREVLINE: Prevention Online
www.health.org

National Institute on Drug Abuse
www.nida.nih.gov

Teen Challenge
www.teenchallenge.com

Office of National Drug Control Policy
www.whitehousedrugpolicy.gov

Index

Picture Credits

page:

13: Associated Press, AP
14: Courtesy of National Institute of Drug Abuse
19: © Bettmann/Corbis
23: © Bettmann/Corbis
29: © Bettmann/Corbis
42: Courtesy of National Institute of Drug Abuse
46: Courtesy of National Institute of Drug Abuse
50: Associated Press, AP
53: © Reuters New Media Inc./Corbis
55: Courtesy of Substance Abuse and Mental Health Services Administration/National Household Survey on Drug Abuse
56: Associated Press, AP

61: Courtesy National Household Survey on Drug Abuse/SAMHSA
63: Courtesy of Substance Abuse and Mental Health Services Administration/National Household Survey on Drug Abuse
66: © Catherine Karnow/Corbis
69: Courtesy of National Institute of Drug Abuse
76: Courtesy of National Institute of Drug Abuse
82: Courtesy of Substance Abuse and Mental Health Services Administration/National Household Survey on Drug Abuse
91: Courtesy of Substance Abuse and Mental Health Services Administration/National Household Survey on Drug Abuse

About the Author

Heather Lehr Wagner is a writer and editor. She earned an M.A. from the College of William and Mary and a B.A. from Duke University. She has written several books for teens on global and family issues and is also the author of *Alcohol* and *Nicotine* in the DRUGS: THE STRAIGHT FACTS series. She lives with her husband and their three children in Pennsylvania.

About the Editor

David J. Triggle is a University Professor and a Distinguished Professor in the School of Pharmacy and Pharmaceutical Sciences at the State University of New York at Buffalo. He studied in the United Kingdom and earned his B.Sc. degree in Chemistry from the University of Southampton and a Ph.D. degree in Chemistry at the University of Hull. Following post-doctoral work at the University of Ottawa in Canada and the University of London in the United Kingdom, he assumed a position at the School of Pharmacy at Buffalo. He served as Chairman of the Department of Biochemical Pharmacology from 1971 to 1985 and as Dean of the School of Pharmacy from 1985 to 1995. From 1995 to 2001, he served as the Dean of the Graduate School and as the University Provost from 2000 to 2001. He is the author of several books dealing with the chemical pharmacology of the autonomic nervous system and drug-receptor interactions, roughly four hundred scientific publications, and has delivered over one thousand lectures worldwide on his research.